THE KOSHER SUTRA

THE *Kosher* SUTRA

SUTRA

Eight Sacred Secrets

for Reigniting Desire

and Restoring

Passion for Life

SHMULEY BOTEACH

HarperOne

An Imprint of HarperCollins*Publishers*

HarperOne

HarperCollins books may be purchased for educational, business, or sales promotional use. For information please write: Special Markets Department, Harper-Collins Publishers, 10 East 53rd Street, New York, NY 10022.

HarperCollins Web site: http://www.harpercollins.com

HarperCollins®, 📖®, and HarperOne™ are trademarks of HarperCollins Publishers

FIRST EDITION

Designed by Jessica Shatan Heslin/Studio Shatan, Inc.

Library of Congress Cataloging-in-Publication Data is available upon request.

ISBN 978-0-06-166835-7

09 10 11 12 13 RRD(H) 10 9 8 7 6

To Cory Booker
Soul-friend and brother who has inspired and uplifted me.
Long ago you told me that G-d had a plan for both us and our
friendship. Here's to that plan coming to fruition and
to you finding your bashert.

&

To David and Sara Berman
Devoted friends who are like family, whose love of children
and constant support of my dream of bringing values to
heal a nation is an ever-present blessing

Contents

THE KOSHER SUTRA

Introduction

Boredom: the desire for desires.
—LEO TOLSTOY

Boring. That's what our lives have become. I should know. I am a reality TV host (not that I'm bragging, since reality TV host rates in the existence continuum just above single-cell amoeba). Can you imagine just how bored you have to be with your own reality when you need to escape into *someone else's* reality? America has become a country of escape artists, with people doing almost anything to flee the monotony of everyday existence and little achieving satisfactory results. Once, we could watch *Star Wars* and be transported to a fantasy land far, far away filled with explosive technology and larger-than-life heroes. When that wasn't enough, we created *People* magazine and celebrity gossip, allowing us to enter the lives of big-screen stars and enjoy small morsels of their glamour. When even that wasn't enough to escape the predictability of our daily grind, we created a new genre of TV so we could invade someone else's reality.

It is the thesis of this book that the death of eroticism in America has presaged the death of nearly everything else. By jump-starting things in the American bedroom and recapturing erotic excitement, we can energize all the other stuff as well.

Why the bedroom? That is where people come to life the most. Or at least, they once did. Today, it's a cold, dark place illuminated not by the heat of two bodies, but by the soft, faint glow of a plasma TV. The one place where you'd expect to find a party, there's nothing but a hangover.

Sex is dying in America. Husbands are often too preoccupied downloading porn to notice the live naked woman next to them in bed. Wives get their erotic charge from shopping in malls rather than slipping on lingerie.

It's a curious phenomenon. Every night in bedrooms across America, millions of married couples go to sleep in the same bed. They are hardy and red-blooded. You would think they would need armed guards to keep their hands off one another. Turns out they can't keep their hands off the remote. They're having sex—on average— about once a week . . . for seven and a half minutes at a time! And that includes the time he spends begging.

And the boredom spills over to areas outside the bedroom.

I took my wife to Times Square on New Year's Eve a few years ago, and together with millions of people we stood in the freezing cold and I stared at a ball. A *ball*. A dropping ball. We were bored to death, or at least we would have been had the cold not killed us off first. How the heck had I bought into this hype? Was I that big a loser? But then, it was New

Year's Eve, and everything around us had told us that we had to have a good time or we would be missing out.

New Year's Eve, the biggest party night of the year, has become a metaphor for modern life. You're supposed to have a terrific time, but most people don't. On TV it seems that everyone is running around drunk and smiling, swinging from the chandeliers, dancing till they drop. But in reality, you go to some friend's party, you do the silly countdown, you sing "Auld Lang Syne," and you go home, wondering whether this is as good as it gets.

We live in the richest country in the world. From the outside it all looks like one big party. People are driving to work in nice cars, running back to nice homes to take care of their kids. Taking great vacations, going to the gym to work out, buying nice stuff at malls. But in reality, these people are going to jobs that don't really engage them and coming home to marriages that no longer captivate them. And their kids, why, they're not even home at all. They're always out with friends. That's how boring they find home life to be.

Every TV show portrays people having a more exciting life than you, having better sex than you, living a more glamorous life than you. Ritchie next door's getting it. So is Bruce, the sexy trainer, who makes a quarter of your salary. They're all gettin' some, except you. So you take a good look at your monotonous life and you feel it's all passing you by. But that's okay. Don't feel bad. Just escape your boring, routine existence with one of thousands of exciting pastimes that can dull the doldrums. So you immerse yourself in *Access Hollywood* in the hope that you can at least live vicariously through the life of some big star, only to discover that it's not all that satisfying to hear daily about Brad and Angelina's adopting the entire nation of Chad. Which makes the whole process even more addictive. Since these mindless escapes are so utterly empty, they don't fill you up, making you insatiable for more. Soon, you're fixated on everyone else's lives but your own.

But the tedium is felt most deeply in the area of intimate relationships. Most married couples are challenged to find something other than a movie to fill their Saturday nights. Wives complain that their husbands become part of the sofa rather than talk to them, and a blaring TV fills in the week-night spaces of our predictable and passionless lives.

What the all-encompassing boredom of American life, and the cheap celebrity banter used to elude it, signify is an unhealthy detachment from the erotic life-force that un-derlies all existence. Eroticism is not a woman with a whip. Even less is it a husband masturbating to porn while his wife is asleep. (That's actually kind of disturbing when you think about it.) Rather, eroticism is the thrilling desire to connect: to know, to explore, to penetrate, and to compre-hend. When our lives are electrified by an erotic pulse, all existence becomes illuminated.

Eroticism is really the psychological and spiritual drive to penetrate the mystery of life and to attach ourselves to the source of all being. When we can consciously access and use our natural impulse for life, we awaken with the realization that everything around us is divinely crafted, and that our own lives, as ordinary as we think they are, contain everything we need to find unending fulfillment. If we can recapture the

erotic flavor of life, then suddenly what you thought was ordinary becomes extraordinary, what you thought was natural
becomes miraculous, and what you thought was commonplace becomes truly unique.

While eroticism is not limited to the sexual, it is through
the sexual that it is most manifest and can best be harnessed.
Understanding the erotic perforce involves fathoming the
sexual. The two are intimate companions such that penetrating the secret of one allows for grasping the hidden aspects
of the other.

Now, America has a contradictory relationship with sex.
On the one hand, sex is everywhere, in advertisements, sports,
magazines, and TV. We use sex to sell beer, spice up our football games, and shore up our Nielsen ratings. It's at the shopping mall in those hot Victoria's Secret display windows. It's
all over our universities. Heck, it's even on our high school
buses!

The one place it isn't is the place you'd most expect to find
it: the American bedroom. One would think that a husband
and wife, immersed in this all-pervasive culture of sex and
more sex would take advantage of their near-constant availability to one another and knock it out of the park. Forget
about it. Studies show that about one third of *all* marriages
in America are utterly sexless. Their sex life is in the marital
morgue. And we're talking for the most part about young
couples, not octogenarians on a Viagra drip. The modern
platonic American marriage is becoming the norm. Of the
twenty families I counseled on my television show, *Shalom
in the Home,* about half had not had sex in more than a year.

And they seemed quite comfortable being in a sexless marriage. Heck, you get more sleep. And you get to be left alone on your side of the bed. The *New York Times* even recently reported a rising trend in new home construction of twin bedrooms for him and her. Husbands and wives are beginning to inhabit two different spheres in the home.

I believe that these two facts—the instant availability of sex in the cultural marketplace versus its increasing nonexistence in the American bedroom—far from being contradictory, are intimately related. The conversion of sex from the highest form of physical intimacy into a marketing commodity designed to move product has purged it of its erotic allure and diluted it to the point where its experience has become uninviting, even unattractive. Sex has lost its potency. It has been miniaturized, trivialized, and has lost its grip on married couples. Worse, eroticism has been vulgarized and cheapened. No longer a pleasurable dream of wild sexual arousal, it is now a pornographic nightmare of misogyny and degradation.

This is not the first book I am writing on sex. My earlier book, *Kosher Sex*, was, thank G-d, an international bestseller that was translated into twenty languages and won rave reviews. I relate this not to brag, but to tell you that the success of my previous book came with a price. Wherever I went, people called me the Sex Rabbi. Whoa! The connotation seemed alarming. *Sexy* Rabbi I could handle. I am, after all, about five foot six, hairy, with a muscular monopack (or as I sometimes describe it, a six-pack surrounded by a cooler). But *Sex* Rabbi? Come on.

But what I found even more troubling was the number of people—both men and women—who told me that they disagreed with the book's emphasis on the importance of sex. "Your problem, Shmuley, is that you make too much of sex. It's really not such a big deal." Hmm, interesting, if sex isn't a big deal, then what is? Shopping? iPhones? ESPN? To a great many people these things are a lot more inviting than sex with their spouses. Madonna is even on record as saying that she finds reading a book in bed a lot more interesting than sex. Sex has become so powerless in the life of the average married couple that it loses out to TV on almost any given night. Imagine that. A real live, hot-blooded man, lying next to a real live, sultry woman, pushed together in bed, naked! And they . . . watch television. But if we trivialize the centrality of sex and eroticism in marriage, what is left to husbands and wives through which they can deeply connect? Discussing politics?

There is a need to recapture the potency of sex and recreate the electricity of desire. Doing so will require fathoming its deeper meaning. If we can recreate the mystery of sex, we can rediscover its erotic allure. And if we rediscover its eroticism, then we can reclaim its passion. And once we reclaim its passion, it will penetrate every aspect of our daily lives. We *can* restore sex to the central place it once occupied in the romantic relationship between man and woman, husband and wife.

Join me on a journey to that rarest of things, namely, a deep understanding of eroticism and how we can use the insights we acquire in recovering the forgotten power of sex. And far from the erotic being something that can only enhance our relationships, it's actually something that can enhance every other aspect of life as well. Sex is the most powerful, engaging, and magnetic aspect of life. Its force is nuclear. And if we can tap into its reserves, we can live our lives at the mountain's summit, never to be deflated by boredom or routine again.

In *Kosher Sex* I discussed how sex could be used to achieve intimacy, how carnal proximity can sew husband and wife together as bone of one bone and flesh of one flesh. In this book, the focus is on using the sexual to achieve the erotic. In our culture we mistakenly do the opposite. We use what passes for the erotic to fuel what passes for the sexual. Couples will watch porn together and tie each other up in handcuffs in the hope that it will spark lust and lead to what is usually very quick and unsatisfying sex. But precisely the opposite is true. The goal of sex is to invite the erotic. The joy of sex leads to the celebration of life. A desire to know one another in the bedroom fuels our desire to know everything that surrounds us outside the bedroom. Our insatiability for each other's bodies leads to an insatiability for each other's spirits. So, we need to uncover the secrets of the erotic mind.

We'll also explore how we can use sex to achieve lasting intimacy, and how we can make sex passionate again. Only by enjoying the proximity and familiarity that flows from a truly intimate connection can the masculine and feminine generate sparks. And once those sparks begin to fly, we'll transfer them from the sexual to the nonsexual, from physical intimacy to emotional oneness, from the bedroom to the kitchen to the living room and beyond. Existence will become richer, life more colorful, everyday events more engaging. Eroticism, while it may be sparked by someone else, is really about discovering one's *own* complexity. It's a moment of self-recognition where a certain void within oneself becomes palpable. It's when the mystery of you becomes more revealed. Intimate interaction with another allows you to get a glimpse into yourself, and it leaves you aching for more. And when you tap into *your* source, and realize the complexity of your being, your eyes are open to the same depth and complexity of all existence and you begin to see beauty everywhere.

On our journey, we'll first focus on the death of sexuality in our time and the forces behind its demise. Then we'll look at how our society came to have such a paucity of understanding of the erotic that erotica is today defined as a sado-masochistic fetish as opposed to a real yearning for the very core of our partner. After that, the eroticization of existence itself becomes our objective, with our goal being to bring out the erotic dimension in every aspect of life.

Get ready, you're about to embark on an erotic ride.

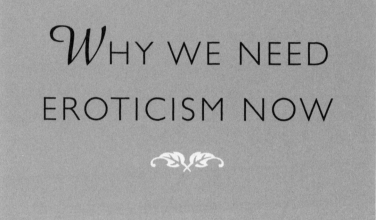

WHY WE NEED EROTICISM NOW

I am in that temper that if I were under
water I would scarcely kick to come to the top.
—JOHN KEATS

A few summers ago my family and I took an RV trip from Oregon to Alaska. It required a whole week of driving through Canada just to get to the Alaska border. For much of that week we were passing through tiny little Canadian townlets in the high reaches of northwest British Columbia. Often people would recognize me from my TV show, *Shalom in the Home*.

I remember a conversation with a married woman who worked as a waitress in a diner. She asked me for my autograph and told me how boring her town was. It was tiny. There was nothing to do. She went on and on. She asked me about the places I had visited. She wanted to travel to destinations that would offer excitement and drama. She seemed sad, and spoke as if life had passed her by. Feeling stuck in a life with nothing to look forward to, she seemed to dream of all the trappings that Hollywood offers—red carpets, paparazzi, private jets.

This story might seem fairly common. A woman from a small city meets someone she watches on TV and is under the impression that his life is so much more exciting. Why can't she be famous?

Of course, she was very wrong about me. Like most married men, my life revolves around being a husband and father. I attend no Hollywood premieres and receive no red-carpet treatment. As far as family life is concerned, I experience most of the same challenges that viewers of my show do, from discipline issues with the kids to the challenge of supporting a large family. I take out the garbage rather than hang out with famous people. I read my kids bedtime stories rather than read about myself in tabloid newspapers. And I come home to the same beautiful woman whom I have, thank G-d, been married to for twenty years, rather than serially dating supermodels. I am not even a D-list celebrity, so there is no Hollywood glamour in my life. But even if she weren't wrong about me, she would still be making a fundamental error about herself.

My waitress was making the tragic mistake of believing that she has to travel somewhere, buy something, or acquire an army of admirers in order to make life exciting. In truth, all she has to do is discover the depth—the hidden spark—that underlies all that surrounds her, and especially the buried treasure that exists just beneath the surface of her own life.

The same applies to people who have lost the passion in their lives not due to any boring routine, but because life has hurt them in some way, however inconsequentially. Candace

was a woman in her early thirties, rapidly climbing the cor-
porate ladder. While delivering a paper on Internet stocks at
an international conference, she was rudely interrupted by
the CEO of a company she was criticizing. He stood up and
launched a diatribe against her. A gentle person by nature, she
was taken aback and didn't know how to respond. Worse, the
CEO had an acid sense of humor. When she didn't respond
to his attack, he cried out, "My company is involved in artificial intelligence, but we take no responsibility for those
whose intelligence is completely artificial." Everyone in the
audience laughed and she felt humiliated. A friend of hers
brought her to see me. "I used to be so passionate about my
work, but now I've lost interest. I want to drop out and do
something else." For Candace, as for the waitress above, running to something new might provide the solution they'd
been searching for.

How can we recapture our passion for living when life is
filled with tall obstacles? And how can we learn what real
passion is as opposed to the fake variety that more often than
not gets us into trouble?

A twenty-nine-year-old woman came to see me in my
office at the prodding of her parents. In the year before the
meeting she had become obsessively religious. Her complete
transformation was causing terrible tension with her family.
She gave away her expensive clothes to the poor and spent
hours a day in prayer. "Why are you doing all this?" I asked
her. "Is your spiritual journey a case of running *to* the light,
as you suppose, or perhaps you are simply running *from* some
terrible darkness?"

She told me her story. "At sixteen I had my first sexual experience. The guy was over forty. At twenty-three, after completing university, I joined a commune that practiced free love. I've slept with about fifty guys. I feel dirtly and I want to cleanse myself of all that. So maybe I am running from something." I then asked the next logical question. "And why did you do all that in the first place?" "I did it," she told me, "because I wanted passion in my life. It made me feel like I was really living."

This woman had mistaken license for passion. Women love bad boys for the same reason. The bad boy lives with a devil-may-care attitude. He breaks the mold, does as he pleases, and exhibits enormous self-confidence in the process. Man, is he sexy. That is, until you become one of the rules he breaks. But none of these escapes will succeed in bringing an authentic erotic quality to life. Here's why.

There are two ways to find excitement in life, the horizontal and the vertical. The horizontal is the most common. It is where, when you get bored of the routine of everyday life, you invent distractions that break the routine. And these distractions come in the form of "horizontal renewal," finding new things in your life to break the tedium. You get tired of where you live, so you move to a new city. You get bored with your job, so you quit and work at a new place. Or you travel, spending much of your year planning your vacation. You're bored on most Sundays, so you go to a shopping mall nearly every weekend and buy a bunch of junk you don't need (which explains why eBay, where you can resell that junk, has become so popular). But it gives you something new to make you feel good about yourself, albeit for a day or two. A friend recently told me about some study that says that the pleasure-factor derived from purchasing a new car lasts about a week. From my own experience, I would say that two weeks is about right. This is why almost all of us trade cars every few years.

Horizontal renewal is insatiable. You grow restless with the person you're married to so you have an affair with a new person who brings along a new body.

One of the most challenging marital cases brought to me involved a young woman, married twelve years, who was having an emotional affair with her car mechanic. The woman was a thirty-eight-year-old mother of four children, a churchgoing Christian. She was smitten with this other man. She sat in my office with her husband. He cried much of the time, said he loved his wife, wanted her back, but she was adamant that she no longer loved him. "I can't go back to this marriage. It's like going back to the grave. I was dead for the last seven years. I accepted that my heart was closed. I would have lived like this for the sake of the children. But Henry has brought me back to life. He's like oxygen to me." When her husband left the room, she told me more. "People look down at Henry because he's a car mechanic. But in truth, he is smart and kind. I really believe he's my soul mate. He's very moral, has a deep sense of right and wrong. He cares about me." She swore she could not give him up. He had become like a drug to her. I pointed out to her that he may, indeed, be moral, but dating a married woman is anything but. And if he really cared about her, he would withdraw from her life long enough for her to determine whether or not she wanted to remain in the marriage or leave, but he would certainly not allow himself to be the cause of the breakup. But she would not listen, and I found myself walking on eggshells. Any perceived criticism of Henry immediately shut her heart. She could not accept the possibility that as soon as this was no longer a fling and instead became a relationship that, after her divorce, he would have to commit to, the circumstances might change and he might not be as interested.

What had happened here was that this wife had tasted of a passion born of horizontal renewal. Surely marriage, with its demands for vertical probing, could never provide the same erotic flavor. A lot of people believe that passion can never exist within the confines of traditional living. Passion can never coexist alongside rules. It is eroded by any kind of institution. You have to break the rules, find new flesh, to rekindle excitement.

But that should not surprise us in an age where the average person grows tired of the book they're reading and starts reading something else before finishing it. Heck, due to the insatiable nature cultivated by horizontal yearning, people can't even watch TV anymore. Instead, they channel surf.

Horizontal renewal is where you deal with the boredom of life by adding new experiences, new travel destinations, new sexual partners, or new possessions in order to compensate for an inner emptiness. Of course, the horizontal expansion doesn't work. You're not really changing anything about yourself. You're just adding new things that you're bound to get bored of after a while, forcing you to start all over again. That's why it's so addictive. Notice that every kind of horizontal expansion designed to compensate for an inner emptiness becomes an addiction: from workaholism, to shopping, to eating, to porn. It all becomes something you can't control.

Nothing can really compensate for a void at the center of your being. You can stuff all the experiences and material objects in the world into that void, but since it is a bottomless pit, you will never fill it up. You'll just feed the beast and become more insatiable. After a while you become a prisoner to those external experiences or objects.

Nearly every day I receive an unsolicited e-mail from a married woman who tells me that her marriage is being destroyed by a husband who is a porn addict. Meredith's case is typical. "Dear Shmuley, my life has become a living nightmare. For the past few months my husband has seemed distant. By day he barely speaks to me. At night, he doesn't touch me. He spends all his time on his computer. One night, when he was asleep, I went on his laptop and was shocked to find thousands of the most disgusting porn images. Thousands and thousands. This is what he was doing with all his time. I woke him up and we had a huge fight. He said he'd done nothing wrong. He didn't cheat on me, he said. Porn is no big deal. I haven't slept in many nights and I'm thinking of leaving him. He puts me down, telling me that I'm hysterical and these are just a bunch of silly pictures and I should calm down. Can you please tell me what you think I should do?" Fascinating. A man expends all his erotic energy on women other than his wife, has nothing left to give her as a woman, and then accuses her of overreacting when she flips out. To be sure, this marriage can and should be salvaged. But that doesn't mean that Meredith isn't justified in feeling so wounded.

When you become addicted to horizontal renewal, then no matter how much you travel, and no matter what you own, you'll still always be bored. Hollywood celebrities—the people the Canadian waitress would look to as leading the most glamorous lives—are usually the emptiest of all. They are so disenchanted with their lives that, amid all the red carpets and jet-setting, they can't remain interested in a marriage or even their career. They hop from relationship to relationship, from bed to bed, from booze to drugs, and finally from rehab to rehab. Only people whose lives are monotonous and empty would need to gas up on drugs to make it all tolerable.

Contrast this with those who are wise enough to fill themselves internally with something completely different: vertical renewal. Vertical renewal is when you abnegate boredom by finding the deeper layers of life, the secrets of existence. It's where, little by little, you scrape away the outer layers of things, revealing their inner dimensions until you discover their essence. You do not seek to mitigate boredom through travel, acquisition, or new flesh. Rather, you find the hidden sparks that exist in your own backyard and your own bedroom.

Notice that the quintessential posture of the living is vertical while the posture of the dead is horizontal. Those who engage in vertical renewal are awake and experience life in all its vitality. But those who are condemned to the desperation of horizontal renewal are dead to life and survive instead on things.

Meredith's porn-addicted husband, who seemed so bored with his wife's body that he needed thousands of new ones to excite him, could have done things very differently. Although he thought he knew everything there was to know about his wife's sexuality, he could have given her an erotic quiz, cajoling her into slowly revealing her deepest erotic fantasies. Women have much more elaborate sexual fantasies than men (read Nancy Friday's *My Secret Garden* and you'll find out for yourself), and discovering their variety and complexity is positively mind-blowing. Had Meredith's husband believed that his wife had infinite sexual layers, he would have stripped off one after another on a nightly basis and given himself and his wife an incredibly powerful erotic charge. Likewise, he could have gotten her to open up about how her sexuality developed when she was a young woman. When did she first experience lust? Who was the first man that exerted such a strong magnetic attraction that she found herself overwhelmed by its pull? In short, he could have opened many secret chambers in his wife's libido that would have been much more thrilling than silly porn. But he took the easier and emptier horizontal road, rather than probing vertically and finding a real gusher. What a foolish man. What a bore.

A young computer programmer came to see me with what seemed to be a simple problem. He wanted to be in a relationship with a woman. He was in his mid-thirties and had already dated, by his own estimate, about eighty women. None of the budding relationships lasted more than about three dates. We were trying to identify the cause of his inability to take a relationship forward when he suddenly volunteered, "Oh, I almost forgot. I have a real problem with porn. You might even say I'm an addict. Been doing it since I was a teenager." I asked him what he had done to try to master the problem. "I went to SA meetings, you know, Sexaholics Anonymous. I was told it was the only thing that could really cure me, group therapy and being honest enough to 'fess up to my addiction, just like an alcoholic or drug addict." I told him that there is a difference between alcohol addiction and porn addiction. "With alcohol we're trying to numb pain, to stop feeling, to experience death. With porn precisely the opposite is the case. We're trying to feel alive. That's what sex is: the ability to feel completely alive. Only, sex has lost its erotic quality, so we turn to porn instead. And that's the secret of why you're not falling in love. For your thrills you've become dependent on variety, on an erotic charge that is defined by horizontal renewal. So when it comes to dating the same woman over and over again, you immediately start getting bored. You need new women to thrill you because you've never learned how to mine the deeper aspects of the same woman."

Those who don't submit to laziness, those who overcome the natural human propensity toward a slow spiritual death, uncover new layers of meaning, new hidden treasures within the same terrain, exciting new facets of the person whom they are in love with, and make life sizzle. The same applies to the rest of life. When Alexander the Great visited Diogenes and asked whether he could do anything for the famed teacher, Diogenes replied, "Only stand out of my light." Alexander was addicted to horizontal renewal. He was insatiable. He would conquer one country, quickly get bored, and move on to another. He conquered the entire earth and still it was not enough. His restless soul knew no peace. But the philosopher Diogenes was an adventurer of the mind. Standing in one place, his life was infinitely more thrilling. He required nothing other than enough light by which to read and imagine.

Diogenes understood the essence of living erotically. For what is Eros, other than the ability to make any situation or person scintillating?

For all our material prosperity and our technological marvels, it still seems that our lives are empty and drab. Life has no fire, our relationships no spark. We're insatiable and don't savor our achievements. We're medicated, materialistic, and morose. Some say we've become shallow and have dedicated our lives to insubstantial pursuits. Others accuse us of being narcissists, too self-absorbed to rise to the level of sacrifice of previous generations. Still others fault our ambition. We have no time for relationships. We're all working too hard. We're driven by a sense of insignificance, insecurity, and fear.

Do you recognize yourself in the description above? All of these things are symptomatic of a more fundamental problem. Simply put, we are not engaged; not by our jobs, not by our marriages, not by our very existence. Even our kids bore us. Why else would we sit them in front of a television or a video game for hours on end rather than playing ball with them or reading them bedtime stories? If we weren't bored, would we be talking about George Clooney's love life or Amy Winehouse in rehab? Would men and women date by going to the movies? Would husbands and wives fantasize about other people when making love to each other? And if life really engaged them, would teenagers experiment with drugs?

The only thing that seems to excite us is the absence of life. Death and tragedy fill the evening news. A terrorist attack will garner a wealth of media coverage; a shooting spree on a college campus will dominate headlines for days. Murder and mayhem, rape and pillage—these are the stuff of our novels and films. Life requires drama to excite, dysfunction to enervate. Marital betrayal will focus our attention infinitely more than honoring its commitment. A man whose wife is leaving him told me the other day that what is compounding the pain of his divorce is how the whole community is now focused on their problems. "It's almost pornographic," he said. "They all want to see the train wreck of our marriage. Their lives are so dull they need my tragedy to live a little."

Boredom is the bane of human existence, the rot that snuffs out all life. If it is true that history is replete with misery and pain, then boredom is certainly a principal cause. Boredom has killed more people, ruined more marriages, and alienated more children from parents than any other catalyst. It is also the source of many of the world's wars. Men with too much testosterone and too few healthy outlets fought each other on bloody battlegrounds to find excitement and adventure. Disemboweling each other provided a respite from an otherwise sedentary existence.

The Talmud summed it up best: "When you have nothing to do, you do what you ought not to do."

For most of us, life quickly settles into an endless cycle of monotonous routine. The drudgery of everyday existence means that most men and women have little to look forward to and accounts for why the entertainment industry

24

in America so dominates all other sectors. Why else would we care whether Britney Spears is wearing underpants or whether Paris Hilton is in jail?

For all too many people the passion for living is quickly lost, the curiosity for existence quickly dissipates. When we first marry we want to know everything about our spouse. But after a few years of marriage, TV has become our surrogate lover. Toward our spouse we adopt the been-there-done-that mentality. The same is true of our jobs. When we begin a new job we will come in early and leave late to impress the boss. But after a few months, our enthusiasm dampens. Getting up in the morning becomes a chore.

This boredom and listlessness extends into other areas of life as well. The colors of the rainbow don't fascinate us as much as they did when we were kids. We are not as interested in sunrises and sunsets. Life loses much of its mystery, awe, and wonder. As kids we ask an endless number of questions. But as we get older, the questions recede. Not because we have found the solutions, but because we are no longer interested in the answers.

I see this with my own kids. Our nine children are basically broken down into two groups: the four teenagers, and the five under age twelve. The latter love skiing with me, hiking, hearing stories, and enjoying nature. But the teens? Motivating them to get out of the house can be like pulling teeth. Hearing that we're going bike riding as a family on a Sunday afternoon will inevitably cause them to come up with an endless number of mystery illnesses that prevent them from participating. "Tatty, I really want to come on that fifty-mile bike ride. What a shame that I contracted leprosy last night and my skin is shedding." Oh really, but you don't look sick to me. "Okay, you're right. The leprosy has passed. But I heard on the news that there's going to be an outbreak of locusts this afternoon, so we're really better off staying inside and listening to our iPods, that is, if we want to be safe."

How did all of life become so uninviting and ordinary? Whereas once upon a time we would look at a snow-covered mountaintop and simply stand back in wonderment, now we either want to climb it to prove our mastery over it, or to build a ski lift on it so we can make money off of it. Life assumes a utilitarian purpose where everything is decided by its usefulness and potential for profit. No wonder that so many marriages crumble as more husbands and wives ask themselves not what they can do for their marriages, but what their marriages can do for them.

But contrary to popular belief, boredom does not stem from a lack of external stimuli. History is replete with examples of kings and queens who were surrounded by incalculable wealth, every kind of novelty, mistresses and lovers, and who were still bored to tears. The lives of our modern Hollywood kings and queens prove the same. A life lived before the paparazzi still cannot rescue them from the feelings of restlessness that are the cause of the destruction of so many artificial Hollywood heroes. Heath Ledger died tragically of an accidental overdose as he tried to numb himself with sleeping pills and antianxiety medication. Marilyn Monroe did the same. Clearly, a life lived in the spotlight did little to engage their energies.

But what, pray tell, is the cause of boredom? What is its essence and what constitutes its life-force?

Life loses its magic when it loses its erotic spark. Eroticism, that thirsty desire to uncover the mystery of life and the complexity of existence, is the liquid that must be injected into our bloodstream. At its core, the erotic is a magnetic pull toward the hidden essence of all that is. The erotic invites us to dive into life, to penetrate its enigma. It is a potent human elixir of curiosity and passion.

When a man makes love to a woman erotically, his passion is felt in every movement, in every thrust. Penetration becomes a desire for fusion. He seeks not to invade her, but to become one with her. He wishes to enter not just a part of her, but all of her. He wishes to be grafted on to her, thereby rendering them inseparable. Even small distances cannot be tolerated. The more she feels his passion and his lust, the more she abandons herself to him. And slowly they become one.

Contrast that with the perfunctory lovemaking that is the hallmark of most marital sex. It consists of husbands and wives going through the motions. He uses her body for friction. She has no core, only body parts. He makes love to aspects of her rather than the core of her being. She feels his detachment. Both end up dissatisfied.

When a man is erotically charged about a woman, he desires to know her in all her ways, not just the sexual. Her breathing becomes interesting to him. He must know her thoughts. Even the color of her fingernail polish has power over him. When he makes love to her, he does not think about other women. Less so does he close his eyes to tune her out. On the contrary, he peers deeply into her eyes as he attempts to penetrate her soul. As they look into each other's pupils, they experience nonverbal communication. Whole paragraphs are exchanged with a simple glance, emotions so powerful that they could never be captured in words.

Those who have experienced this level of soulful erotic communication know exactly to what I refer. It is, to be sure, a rare event, but utterly unforgettable when it does occur.

The erotically charged man is constantly interrogating the woman he loves as to her thoughts, her dreams, her whims, and her pain. A demon has grabbed hold of him. No matter how much exposure he has to the woman in question, it is never enough. Eroticism has made him insatiable. That's why eroticism, while not limited to lovemaking, is most often expressed through physical love, because sex, as the Bible says, is the highest form of knowledge.

I once counseled a married couple who complained that their sex life was dead. Both husband and wife said that they had little passion for one another. I gave them a homework assignment. "I want you, Morris, to give your wife a long sensual massage, lasting an hour, three nights in a row. With each consecutive night, I want you to enter more and more forbidden zones. First night, make it clean. But the third night, it should be downright dirty. There are two rules. No sex and no orgasm."

They followed my advice, but it failed to bring them closer or make things more exciting. The following week when we spoke, the husband told me, "I felt like a massage therapist. I didn't see the point. After fifteen minutes of touching her and seeing her get aroused, I was desperate to have sex with her. The fact that I couldn't was frustrating and created distance. What was the purpose of the exercise anyway?" I replied, "Morris, the purpose of the exercise was to enhance eroticism. It was to excite you to such heights of arousal and unrequited desire that you *live with your lust* for your wife instead of purging it from your system by having unfulfilling sex. As you go through the boring and monotonous motions of your empty sex life with your wife, you become utterly oblivious to her mystery. You *do* her. And she gets done. The purpose here was to arouse her night after night and for you to watch her come alive in all her feminine glory without any of that erotic energy being allowed to escape through climax. Suddenly, you're looking at a woman writhing in agony. You look at her and you conclude that this is a woman you scarcely know. Don't you get it? Sex is not supposed to be about purging yourself of an urge. It's designed to make you want her more, not less.

"And for you, Cynthia, the purpose was to see your husband as the key to unlocking your latent eroticism, bringing out desire and lust in you that you scarcely knew existed. All of this would lead to your both wanting *not to have sex* with one another, but to *explore* each other, to know each other in every way, not just the physical. The purpose was to create limitless curiosity.

"But it didn't work for you, and here's why. Both of you are too goal-oriented in sex. You think that in marriage you're supposed to have sex. Let's get it over with. Hey, this massage is getting me horny. Let's get this urge out of our system so we can go back to being married. Little did you realize that living erotically is the best kind of marriage."

Wherever it is taught and discussed, the story of Adam and Eve in the Garden of Eden has an erotic subtext. Whether it is the fact that the two are described as being naked and unashamed, or whether the focus is on the seductive qualities of the serpent as he slowly corrupts the otherwise innocent Eve, the story is infused with erotic overtones. This is no accident. The Bible wishes to convey that erotic desire is, as Sigmund Freud said, the life-instinct and the source of all knowledge.

Notice that when Adam and Eve are first created, they are like children. They walk around naked like children, and they have a child's curiosity about their environment. They frolic in a garden of infinite possibility. They have no painful experiences in their past and no disappointment. Their relationship is erotic precisely because they hold nothing back. They haven't been hurt yet, so they have no defense mechanism. Their innocence is the secret of their power. They invest themselves in each other completely and fully. They are not afraid of being let down. Wow. That's powerful.

We who have so degraded eroticism by making it into something with whips and chains cannot accept that the eroticism inherent in the relationship between Adam and Eve is inextricably bound with their innocence. They are in a brand-new world, they are young and naïve, and they want to know everything. Their curiosity is the real kernel of the story. Immersed in a beautiful garden that would quickly bore the rest of us for its lack of TV, magazines, and Internet, they want to know every tree, every bird, and every rosebud.

Most of all, they want to know each other. Hence, there is no shame in their nakedness. Whereas for us nakedness is either a form of embarrassment for our unattractive bodies, or a source of guttural arousal, for them, nakedness was the source of intellectual, emotional, and spiritual connectedness. Their nakedness is symbolic of the absence of any barrier. They are utterly exposed and uninhibited.

G-d tells them that they may eat of every tree in the Garden, save one. And why does G-d put one tree off limits? Because forbiddenness enhances eroticism. It is the woman that a man *cannot* have after whom he lusts the most. Often I hear of men and women who had a great sex life prior to marriage that quickly settled into a boring routine once they lived together as husband and wife. Once it all became legal, it wasn't as powerful.

By making something off-limits to them, G-d is teaching Adam and Eve to lust, to hunger, to want, to desire. Humankind's natural inclination is to seek to master, to conquer. G-d is teaching Adam and Eve to resist that temptation. There are things in life that will always be off-limits and therefore instill lifelong yearning. There are aspects of the woman to whom you are married that you will never fathom, dimensions of her personality that will forever prove inaccessible. So you'll never get bored because part of her is forbidden and unknowable. You cannot know her thoughts. You cannot know her fantasies. Nor can you ever completely possess her heart. She will always be attracted to strangers, even if you are the most devoted man in the world. A woman is sexually insatiable. G-d is teaching Adam and Eve that they will never have complete dominion over the earth and they will never have complete dominion over each other, either. They will always hunger for more.

Everyone knows that Virginia Woolf committed suicide by drowning. But fewer know that she wrote a short story that in some ways can be seen as prophetically predicting her own demise. The story is called "The Legacy." It is about a man, Gilbert Clandon, in the aftermath of his wife's tragic death. His wife, Angela, leaves her husband a fifteen-book set of her diaries. In the diaries, Gilbert finds reference to a stranger called "B.M." with whom Angela would discuss politics. As the diaries progress, she writes more about B.M. and the time she spends with him until it becomes clear that they are lovers. B.M. apparently kills himself when Angela can't make a decision to leave her husband and Angela is devastated. Her last entry is simply this: "Have I the courage to do it too?" Her husband, who all along thought that she was killed by accidentally being hit by a car, comes to understand that she threw herself in front of the car and that she did so from the pain of knowing that she could never again be with her lover. The moral of the story is that, as it turns out, a husband who thought he knew his wife after so many years of marriage knew next to nothing about her. He did not know her passionate needs; he was oblivious to her sexual side. He behaved as though he were married to a mannequin. The real woman underneath escaped his glance. But how many other women are there who would fit into the same category, living with men who have never fathomed their erotic depths?

Jody and Wayne came to me for counseling. Their marriage suffered from a poor sex life. Jody especially was disheartened by the boredom of the bedroom. She said everything she proposed to liven things up was rejected by her husband. "Like what?" I asked. Wayne chimed in. "Let me answer so as not to embarrass her. She wanted us to videotape ourselves having sex." "And why didn't you?" I asked. "Well, because there has to be something better than making sex into a spectacle," he said. "I think that what our sex life needs is more romance, not exhibitionism. We need more love, not more sex." Wayne went on to explain that for him sex was not something carnal or physical. It was about love and connectedness. So why make it so material, so much about the body? It should be less physical and more emotional.

I spoke up. "It's interesting to see what different poles you're both coming from. You, Wayne, want more romance, because for you the major problem in the marriage is a feeling of rejection. You don't feel loved. You feel that your wife compares you to other men who have more to offer. To feel loved is to feel special, to be unique, and you crave your wife's affirmation. But for you, Jody, the problem is the opposite. Your husband smothers you with affection. You already feel special. But the smothering has become suffocating. The lack of oxygen has extinguished the fire. What you want is to feel alive. And what raw sex and passion do is make you feel alive. You're both right; both passion and intimacy are essential ingredients of marriage. But where you're wrong, Wayne, is in your denigration of the body. For you, carnal love is beneath emotional love. And this is because you view love through a false dualistic model that says that the soul and the heart are special, but the body is just the casing for the two. It's not. The body is sacred. And the heated sex life of a husband and wife in love is glorious and makes them feel connected. Your wife has every right to want to feel alive, and to want you to be the one who makes her experience such intensity of emotion."

Wayne was making the mistake of so many spouses, slowly killing off his wife's libido, extinguishing her fire, in the belief that real love was found only in romantic feeling and not in ecstatic passion.

I believe that husbands do this subconsciously out of fear that they can't measure up to their wive's real erotic needs. The fact is that, contrary to popular belief, women are much more sexual than men. Their sexuality is rooted in their core emotions. And their sexual organs are internal, not external like a man's. It's not something apart from them. Sexuality is central to their very makeup. For men sex is an act of doing. For women, it's an act of being. Men are uniorgasmic. After sexual climax they're all but dead, which is why the French call the male orgasm *Le Petite Mort*, "the little death." Call the morgue. This guy is finished. But women are multiorgasmic. They ascend into a sexual zone that can last the whole night. Their sexuality takes a bit longer to launch, but once ignited the rockets take over. It's much deeper and longer lasting than a man's. And in the face of such intensity, most husbands fear that they can't measure up. So they make sex a quickie affair that barely gets their wives going. It is entirely possible that men subconsciously kill off their wives' libidos with really bad sex as a way of not having to satisfy them sexually. Men also want to be lazy in bed. The woman who is unaware of the degree of her sexual desire, because it has never been aroused by her husband, does not need to be satisfied. So the fearful man finishes before his wife ever gets going.

A woman's sexuality is subtle. Her arousal is devoid of bells and whistles. It's a fire within a coal that must be fanned into a flame. When a man spends hours making his wife feel desirable and engages in long periods of foreplay, he ignites her fuse and their mutual pleasure is potent. But after years of neglecting a woman's sexual needs, her body goes cold and her fire is slowly extinguished. It becomes concealed and harder to access. Men kill off their wives' libidos and instead of attention he gives her credit cards. And she stupidly takes the bait, sublimating her desire for intimacy for acquisition. Shopping now provides her an erotic thrill. Instead of a passionate night of foreplay, she's content going to the mall to buy shoes and jewelry.

In the 1993 movie *Indecent Proposal* Robert Redford plays a polished billionaire who offers a happy but financially struggling couple a million dollars if the wife will spend a night with him. They accept, but soon find their love tested by the conflicts of the bargain. Woody Harrelson plays the husband who is emasculated by the night of passion his wife, played by Demi Moore, has with Redford. The manifestation of his wife's passion makes him love her more than ever before. She is now mysterious, forbidden, and utterly erotic. But it also crushes his ego. How could he possibly satisfy her? She is the woman that everyone wants. Does she compare him to the suitor, can he measure up to the gilded paramour, and worse, is the Redford character in reality the better man? Finally, although they promised each other never to discuss the evening, he cannot help but confront his wife with the terrible question. "Did you enjoy it?" he demands. "Was it pleasurable? I have to know." And when he presses her and she reluctantly says, "Yes," the answer devastates him. He spirals into a terrible pit of self-doubt and disquiet, further emasculating him in his wife's eyes, and further alienating the woman he loves, until she leaves him for the other man. A woman like this is the thrill and the horror of any man. Is it any great mystery, then, that most men avoid the possibility of awakening their wives' insatiable desire by turning her into a much more casual best friend?

A woman is like the sea, bursting with life, at times calm and soothing, and at other times stormy and tempestuous. Like the sea, which swells up and recedes, a woman's libido is regulated by a cycle, making her even more mysterious. No man has ever quite figured a woman out. Even Sigmund Freud threw his hands up, writing after decades of inquiry that he was unable to answer the simple question of what it is that a woman wants. But the man is irresistibly attracted to the raw power of the feminine. He sets out to possess her. But little does he know that a woman is like a secret: once revealed the secret loses its potency. Once a woman is fully possessed, she is no longer as desirable. Her attractiveness is diminished. A woman is like a film negative that when exposed to light slowly loses its color.

The overexposure of the feminine in our time has likewise diminished eroticism. Too much cleavage, too much flesh, too much casual sex has all served to make women too available.

In the short term exposed flesh spawns greater desire. But it is desire that cannot last. It quickly dissipates and men become bored of women.

Men have not learned how to reconcile what seems to them an outward contradiction. Women seem so erotic before you get to know them. But the longer the relationship lasts, the more boredom sets in. The sea pulls into itself everything that draws close. It is infinitely deep; it can never be filled. Its depths can never be fully fathomed. A woman wants her man to desire her intensely. She wants his attention completely. And like the sea's refreshment, she has waves of pleasure to offer in return. But lacking the same depth as women, when men are drawn into that sea, they choose to be snorkelers rather than deep-sea divers. They look at everything from on top. They study skin and body parts. But they rarely unmask their wives' erotic nature. They refrain from erotic conversations. They don't give their wives' long erotic massages that slowly manifest the depth of her arousal.

The history of relationships has been that the female need for attention has rarely been matched by the male attention span. Men get bored after a short while. And then they wonder why the adoring and fawning woman they love suddenly turns into an icy stormy sea. The ferocious sexual power possessed by the woman is transformed into anger that burns rather than heat that comforts. In the same way that no land storm is ever as ferocious as one at sea, so the saying goes, "Hell hath no fury like a woman scorned."

Henrietta came to me for counseling alone. Her husband, Trevor, would not join her. They were both in their second marriage. She complained that Trevor was a great date but a terrible husband. Before they married he showered endless attention on her, but once they married he was cold and detached. She said she was frustrated and lonely. I called Trevor and arranged to see him. He came reluctantly. "Yes, it's true I am withdrawn in this marriage," he admitted. "But the fault lies with my wife. She puts so much pressure on me, so I react by withdrawing. She is always angry and says such nasty things." I asked him why his first marriage fell apart. "Because my wife had a terrible temper." "Do you detect a pattern here?" I asked him. "All these women you're with are angry. Could it be something you're doing, or not doing? Could it be that all the affection you engendered on the part of both these women was turned against you because of your neglect?" But no, he couldn't see it. The anger was theirs. He was the victim.

There is nothing more attractive, more seductive, and more desirable than a stormy female lover. But that stormy, volatile sexual temperament can challenge men like nothing else. Since the male inability to fully possess a fiery woman leads them to question their innate masculinity and hence, their manhood, men will often marry a passionate woman but slowly transform her into a docile and compliant housewife who is content to settle for a small flicker of passion. But often a woman will rebel and not go quietly into that dark night.

In the early nineties, I interviewed Shere Hite, the world-famous sex researcher, at the Oxford Union. She told me that the single most important finding of her "Hite Report on Male Sexuality" was the discovery that over 80 percent of men do not marry the women whom they are most passionately in love with or attracted to. Rather, they pass over that woman in favor of the woman with whom they have the most in common. When it comes to matters of love and sex, husbands are afraid of fires that burn too brightly.

I saw this exact scenario playing out in the marriage of Joel and Tracy when they came to see me on a hot summer night. Tracy was thirty-four and beautiful, but she looked like the living dead. She had a gaunt expression, lifeless features, and didn't once smile. Joel was nervous and fidgety. He asked to speak first, which was just as well because his wife seemed to lack even the energy for human communication. He told me that they had been married for ten years. He admitted that he had utterly neglected his wife as he worked hard to build a business. He confessed to not hearing her when she spoke, not answering her when she questioned, and doing very little to satisfy her sexually. It all changed when one day, suspicious, he snooped on her e-mail account and discovered that she was having an online affair with a man she met on a dating Web site. Joel went crazy. He confronted his wife, and when she confessed that she had fallen in love with this other man, he started pulling out his hair and beating his chest with his fists. He extracted the man's address and sent him a note threatening to harm him if he ever again contacted his wife. He told me he brought his wife to see me in the hope that I could make things better between them. Getting Tracy to speak was like pulling teeth, but when she finally did she told me that it took ten years of marriage to kill her completely. She had become numb to life, dead to the world.

She no longer felt her beating heart. And she lived like that for ten years, content to be alive only as a mother. But then this stranger got her to turn on her webcam and told her she was beautiful. He complimented her, listened to her, and they became online lovers. She explained that the reason she looked so terrible was that she now accepted that her lover was lost to her and she was back to being dead.

Here you have the American marital tragedy in full color. A husband marries a young and vibrant woman, decides that real excitement in life will come from making money and buying things—horizontal renewal—and slowly kills off his wife's deeper layers—vertical renewal —until all that's left is the empty husk of a human being. A riddle had been unraveled, a mysterious woman had been revealed to the point of emptiness, and stultifying boredom was the result. That is, until another man came along and reintroduced an erotic spark. And suddenly, her husband, seeing his wife's deeper layers, that inner yearning for Eros, wanted to reclaim her. No wonder that studies show that the first reaction from a husband upon discovering that his wife is having an affair is to want to have sex with her. A woman who was so ignored by the man in her life that she had to find passion with someone else is revealed to be someone utterly unpredictable and mysterious. And her husband yearns for her anew. Her husband also finds great pleasure in repossessing something he thought he lost.

My friend Carol works in advertising. Last year she was experiencing the slows in her job; she told me that she was so bored that she could hardly get up in the morning. She thought what she needed was to leave that job and start something new. However, because the job paid so well and offered excellent benefits, she endured the boredom for the compensation.

One day as she was making coffee, she heard from behind one of the dividers that her own secretary was making a bid for her job. Carol was furious. Alarm bells went off in her head and she began to work much harder. "It wasn't just fear," she told me. "I genuinely rediscovered a passion for my work. The fact that the job could be taken away from me made it new to me all over again. When I came in the next morning, it was like coming in for the first time ever. I was determined. And now, every time I start to get bored, I just remember that at any moment this job could be lost. And there it is—brand new!" The same applies to many husbands and wives in marriage. It's the discovery that they can never fully know, never fully possess their spouse that makes them passionate about winning them over anew.

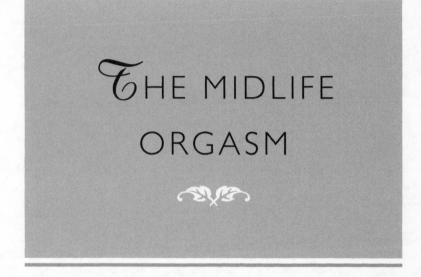

THE MIDLIFE ORGASM

When you're in love, it's the most glorious
two-and-a-half days of your life.
　　　　　　　　　　—RICHARD LEWIS

𝒯o live erotically is to recapture our fascination with the small stuff. It is to experience life's magnetism and pull. To live erotically is to wish to make love to life itself.

Notice that, when it comes to lovemaking, the erotic charge is lost the moment orgasm is felt. Orgasm is a purging of erotic buildup. The same is true of life. Men and women who once seemed to be so enamored of life, now go through the everyday motions of existence robotically and predictably. The reason is the same. *They have orgasmed in their lives.* They have experienced what they believe is a peak, and now, after the peak, there is precious little to look forward to.

While I was writing this book, a monumental study was published by researchers from Warwick University in Britain and Dartmouth College in the U.S. They analyzed data on two million people from seventy nations. What they found was an extraordinarily consistent pattern in terms of depression and happiness levels. From Australia and Italy to Nicaragua and

Azerbaijan, they witnessed how the midlife crisis was slowly becoming a universal phenomenon. People were happy at the beginning of their lives but became depressed beginning in their forties, with age forty-four being the worst year of all.

As the *Daily Mail* in Britain reported, many previous studies had suggested psychological well-being remained relatively flat and consistent as we age. But the new study suggested otherwise.

Using a sample of a million Britons, researchers found both men and women faced their biggest dip in happiness at 44, regardless of marital status, wealth or children. In the U.S., by contrast, there was a big difference between the sexes, with unhappiness peaking at about 40 for women and 50 for men. Warwick's Professor Andrew Oswald said signs of mid-life depression are found in all kinds of people. Some suffer more than others, but in our data the average effect is large. It happens to men and women, to single and married people, to rich and poor, and to those with and without children. He said that what caused the U-shaped curve was unknown, but added: "It looks from the data like something happens deep inside humans."

Well, let the mystery stand no more. I'll tell you exactly what happens. We orgasm. We climax. We peak. We see our lives as reaching its apogee in our forties and then, somehow, the life is beat right out of us. We feel as if our dreams are shattered and our youth squandered. The erotic spark is lost. We become the proverbial man who is comatose on the bed after about ten minutes of sex with his wife and one unsatisfying climax. That's as good as it gets. It wasn't erotic. It wasn't exciting. And it wasn't enough to awaken anything deeper. It was a life lived in the hollows.

I see this kind of burnout all the time. So many good, precious people are just shells of their former selves. They are lifeless, vacant, and often bitter. Life has put them through the rinse cycle and they come out shriveled and shrunk.

They move through life like a passing shadow. Few things animate them. Even their kids don't seem to excite them. They long ago stopped living and now merely subsist. They get by. They pay their bills. And thank G-d for TV, YouTube, and sporting events. At least they have something to look forward to. Their bodies are intact and even healthy. But the spark of the divine has ceased to flicker within. The routine of life and the pain of everyday struggle slowly snuffed out their spirit.

For men, we used to call this a midlife crisis. It is no longer so. Today it is something entirely different. A crisis means that you have hit a wall in your life. Your professional aspirations have been frustrated. You feel like a failure, like life has broken you. But for today's men it's not about a crisis. It's about sheer, unadulterated boredom. They don't look for the blonde and the Porsche. That would require far too much effort. It would presuppose that they feel still feel an inner surge of energy. It would mean that they would have to woo a woman again. Nah. It's easier to find the blonde in Internet porn and the Porsche on a TV ad. They prefer the couch to an affair and a beer to kinky sex. Life can do them no more harm because they have already died within.

Take a man in his forties who played the field while in his twenties, had a lot of girlfriends, and then "settled down" in his thirties. He is now into his first decade of marriage. He has two kids. He loves his wife but he feels bored in his relationship. He feels tied down by domestic responsibilities. His hair is thinning; his paunch is expanding. He struggles to have his trousers stay up as his belly protrudes. Professionally, he has peaked. He has a good job, but cannot really look forward to any serious advancement beyond where he already is. As far he is concerned, his life has climaxed. He has already peaked. The vitality of his once pent-up potential has been spent. His lust for life has been expunged. He has nothing important to look forward to. He longs for his lost youth, but too late. To his mind it is gone. Hence, he no longer really lives life so much as escapes it. Like a man who quickly falls asleep right after sexual orgasm, this man spends the rest of his life asleep as well. When he comes home, he plunks himself in front of the TV. His children speak to him, but he doesn't hear them. He wife hugs him, but she cannot reach him. They have sex rather than make love. Her libido sleeps during the experience. He is oblivious to her feelings of neglect and pain. He becomes obsessed with professional sports as he lives vicariously through the feats of his favorite heroes. And so, the erotic energy of their marriage is lost.

The same is true of so many women who also look into a mirror and see a ghost of their former selves. In place of a smile they see lines. In place of a glow they see wrinkles. They wonder whether they married the right man, even as simple logic dictates that a good marriage is based primarily not on whom you marry but how you treat each other *after* you marry. They, too, have peaked; they, too, have climaxed;, and they, too, have had their life's orgasm. And it's downhill from there.

I once counseled a woman who confessed to me that whenever she and her husband had sex, which was about once a month, she always cried herself to sleep afterward. She did not do so because the sex was bad, although it was awful. Less so did she cry because she felt her husband didn't love her, because she was sure he did. Rather, she mourned her own demise. She was once passionate and alive. And now, she and her husband were dead.

But the same can be true of even teenagers. So many young kids are zombies. They seem energy-less and robotic. The hallmark of youth was once an inexhaustible reservoir of energy. This is no longer true. These kids have peaked at fifteen. It's downhill for the next five years until they emerge from their cocoon and come back to life. They have lost their innocence. They represent Adam and Eve *after* they have been expelled from the Garden. They have been exposed to too much, have internalized corruption at too young an age, and they, too, have peaked. They turn to street drugs for the artificial high that real life cannot afford.

The solution is to learn to *live* erotically, to bring erotic excitement and interest to every area of life. Erotic living is achieved through the constant buildup of erotic energy without allowing it to dissipate. There are many ways to achieve this high station. But all are built around the idea of enhancing erotic consciousness without release. In America, our entire lives are built around *achieving* erotic release. Americans hate tension. Inner peace is what we crave. And we do almost anything to find a false sense of calm. Americans prefer to be dead than to be alive. We take antianxiety medication to feel numb. We down antidepressants to blunt pain. We take sleeping pills to fall asleep. Heck. We even medicate hyperactive children as a less gruesome form of modern lobotomy. And surrounding it all are the tens of millions of corpses that slink down for hours of TV watching every single night—mind-numbing, stupid, idiotic TV that blights the brain and suffocates the spirit.

If we could just learn to foster erotic interest without release, then our curiosity and longing for all that surrounds us would be immeasurably enhanced. In marriage, as an example, this can be achieved through learning to have lovemaking sessions that do not lead to orgasm. Sex without orgasm over a period of, say, a week, leads to significant erotic enhancement that is not diluted by disappointing climax. Erotic steam is built up through sex without sexual release. The more we make love to our spouse and prolong it by refraining from orgasm, no matter how much we feel we want it, the more we awaken the erotic energy within. After a few nights of practicing restraint, our entire world changes. We begin to store huge reservoirs of energy and never get tired. We wake up early and never feel drained. We love our spouse more deeply than ever before because every night we are connecting with them without purging the desire from our heart. Our conversation with others changes as our curiosity for life increases. Whereas before the conversations were perfunctory and practical, they now spring from a deep desire to know and understand all that surrounds us. Our curiosity for life becomes insatiable, our enthusiasm for knowledge limitless, our desire to connect with everything around us unquenchable.

In his twentieth-century classic, *The Closing of the American Mind*, Professor Alan Bloom of the University of Chicago maintains that when he first started teaching in the 1950s, the students would arrive fueled by a powerful desire to know. They had, he claims, an erotic spark. They were curious, they were driven, they were alive. They knew they were looking for something, but they did not quite know what. They were motivated, Bloom says, by unsatisfied Eros, unrequited lust. Students often arrived virginal. Premarital sex was condemned. And their unsatisfied erotic tension drove everything they did. But after the sexual revolution of the 1960s, when sex—and lots of it—between teens became commonplace, Bloom says he saw a noticeable dissipation of student curiosity. By the time these students arrived at college, they suffered already from partial burnout. Life had no surprises, its biggest surprise of all having already been experienced. The dissipation of physical lust had likewise diminished their intellectual yearning. They had lost the itch to know. They knew far too much already. The craving had been satisfied, the tension had been released. And a new generation of students found an erotic charge in alcohol instead, which remains the case until today.

As a marriage counselor I see the truth of this insight in everyday life. When a husband and wife are separated by distance—he or she is traveling, say, on business—they often grow more interested in one another and their lust for one another increases. Not just physically, but even intellectually. Not being able to have his wife's body, he often begins to enjoy her mind. He may even, if he does not dissipate his desire through masturbation, begin to ask his wife to reveal her fantasies to him over the phone so that he can feel closer to her. Likewise, a wife, in missing her husband, may share with him intimacies of the heart and mind that would otherwise be ignored in favor of the practical responsibilities of everyday life. Now, this deepening of the relationship is not merely due to the famous adage that "absence makes the heart grow fonder." Rather, their inability to satiate their mutual lust leads to deeper longing.

There is a further consideration. Bloom's insight about the loss of student Eros captures how central innocence is to eroticism and how it leads to Eros's loss. The reason that we have not reaped the benefits of these practices, like sex without orgasm, is that Western sexuality is so goal-oriented—so strongly focused around sexual climax—that most of us scarcely know the benefits of a *means-oriented* sexuality. And it's killing both our marriages and our general enthusiasm for life. *Life is not meant to climax*. Climax is death.

Reorienting your life away from a strict goal-orientation to a means-orientation is the very beginning of recapturing eroticism in your life. Eroticism is all about arousal, all about building toward climax *without achieving it*. In other words, eroticism is a recognition of the infinity of life and its endless nature. There is no climax, there is no summit. There is only an endless journey of accelerating passion.

Changing our lives from a goal- to a means-orientation would bring back the curiosity and passion that is the very stuff of the erotic spark. Take our jobs as an example. All too many of us work in order to advance or work in order to earn money. But if we were to work in order to maximize our productive capacity for creative output, we would achieve those ends, but would also enjoy the journey. We would have real relationships with our coworkers whom we no longer saw as competitors, and companionship and friendship would be fostered in the office. We would take greater pleasure in the smaller details that often frustrate us because, no longer focused on the next step, we would appreciate how those details slowly build a larger portrait.

Is this not the case with how we parent? Why do we derive so much more satisfaction from raising our children than doing our jobs? To be sure, the fact that we love our children is an important cause. But it's really the *effect* of that love that makes all the difference. Because we love our children and want to enjoy the experience of watching them grow up, we don't rush to the finish line. We don't wait around hoping they're off to college and out of the house. On the contrary, we delay that day. We are means-oriented in raising children, and it shows in how focused we are on details. With our two-year-old, my wife and I call each other up all the time to share the cute things he says and the mess he makes with spaghetti in his hair. The same is true with our older children. I often just watch my teen kids talking to each other because I find it fascinating to see the slow development of their individual and unique characters. And if we could just bring some of this means-orientation to other areas of life, we could rediscover the latent erotic spark. You've heard this before, but now you understand why, we have to learn to live in the present, to enjoy the present. The focus on the future is not only wrong because it ensures that we cannot enjoy the moment, but because its future-focused goal-orientation is all about orgasming, climaxing, finishing, and losing our interest in life. The height of knowledge is to know that you cannot know. There is no culmination. There is no end. All is infinite.

Here's an interesting concept for you to get your head around: orgasming internally. Orgasm is usually seen as something that happens outside the body. Its deficiency: when all that sexual steam is expelled, your lust is diminished. But what if orgasm took place internally? Living erotically includes orgasming internally and not allowing our sexual steam to escape. Rather than have an orgasm, which involves the expiation of sexual passion through ejaculation, the orgasmic energy is not expunged. Instead, it is rechanneled internally, thereby heightening overall erotic interest. Okay, I admit. This is easier said than done. But practical applications are readily identifiable. Indeed, the multiorgasmic nature of women is the most practical demonstration. When a woman is aroused by her husband to the heights of sexual ecstasy, her sexual climax serves to heighten, rather than deaden, her sexual interest. With each sexual peak she experiences greater sexual abandon. She is orgasming internally. The sexual buildup is released inside, thereby creating greater intensity rather than being diminished. But this comes about specifically through the continued stimulation of her husband. Even as he brings her to climax, he continues to stimulate her erogenous zones. Not content to simply push her over the threshold, he ensures that, once there, she actually soars. And the intensity of the experience ensures that the rocket thrust of her boosters is directed *back into the experience* rather than begin expended outside.

For men, the experience is somewhat different. Since orgasm involves ejaculation, a literal expunging of the sexual elixir, climaxing internally cannot involve physical orgasm. Rather, for a man internal climax is defined as a mind orgasm, explosions of incredible erotic power that go off like depth charges in the brain. The mind orgasm is where a man, brought to the heights of erotic desire by continued sexual buildup and by refraining from sexual release, has all his erotic pleasure redirected away from the genitals so that it is released in the mind. Like a volcano whose fiery pressure is all channeled upward until it can no longer be contained, it erupts in a fiery inferno of passionate pleasure. Physical release is not even contemplated because the erotic zone is no longer in his lower regions. On the contrary, everything is now focused in his brain. As he passionately touches or makes love to the wife he desires, he is engaged in the mental quest for knowledge the entire time. He probes her deeply for information. He asks her, with intense directness, to describe the sensations her body is experiencing with what he is doing to her. He asks her, as he grabs her ferociously and draws her close, to describe all the men she is attracted to and all who are attracted to her. He demands—not asks, but demands—that she reveal her deepest sexual secrets to him. He is insatiable to know her. He devours her with his mind. Cheap, tawdry, sexual release is the last thing he wants. On the contrary, he intuitively delays climax in order to prolong the mind orgasm. He mines her for information the way that an interrogator might squeeze life-and-death information from his prisoner. He will die if he does not know.

This is the inner release of the internal orgasm. He explodes cerebrally and the erotic steam generated by the explosion is channeled back into his bloodstream, making him crave and yearn for the woman in his wife ever more deeply.

Living erotically is possible for all who wish to experience life at the mountain's summit rather than the valley's trough. All it takes is to redirect our sexual passion internally rather than externally. In the following chapters, I will continue to show you how with the eight secrets of eroticism.

The First Secret: Innocence

There is no aphrodisiac like innocence.
—JEAN BAUDRILLARD

*E*roticism is a passionate, fiery stew comprised of eight ingredients. And it is these eight components that make the sexual connection between a husband and wife electrifying. When we understand how these operate in the sexual sphere, we can then extrapolate beyond them to the nonsexual as well. These energies can be harnessed to provide unending passion in every aspect of life. The first is innocence.

Our first introduction to the human body is through Adam and Eve where, in their original primal state, they are "naked and unashamed" (Genesis 2:25). There is something lofty about the human body in its pristine condition that is only later tainted by Adam and Eve's sin. Having done nothing wrong, they had nothing to hide. Sexuality in the Garden is transparent. However, immediately after they dine at *Bistro de Tree de Knowledge*, they are consumed by shame and must hide themselves:

Then the eyes of both were opened, and they knew that they were naked; and they sewed fig leaves together and made themselves aprons . . . the man and his wife hid themselves from the presence of the LORD God among the trees of the garden. But the LORD God called to the man, and said to him, 'Where are you?' And he said, 'I heard the sound of thee in the garden, and I was afraid, because I was naked; and I hid myself.'

(Genesis 3:7–10)

What happened here? One moment they're running around stark naked, and the body is nothing to be ashamed of. They celebrate the sexual side of their nature, which is neither sinful nor an affront to G-d. The next moment, the body has become something lowly and sex something to be hidden in the closet.

Well, the aprons were not intended for role-playing, and the hiding was not an erotic game. Maimonides explains that the nature of Adam and Eve's sin was that the objective became subjective. When Adam and Eve were naked in the Garden, they related to each other as two people without pretension, which is what nakedness connotes. When Adam looked upon Eve in her original pristine state, the first thought that crossed his mind was not, *Nice hooters*, but *Nice heart*. His attraction to her was based on the objective standards of Eve's actions rather than on the subjective standard of her looks. He was attracted to his wife holistically, focusing on the totality of her being rather than on a collection of body parts. It was the attraction of masculine to feminine, magnetic pole to magnetic pole. And because Eve felt that her husband loved *all* of her, rather than just her legs or her genitals, there was no need to cover up. She did not feel judged by a single dimension of her being. There was nothing to hide. She wasn't ashamed of her body and she wasn't self-conscious about her looks. She didn't compare her cheekbones to models she saw in magazines. She didn't look at her legs and see short stubs or lines on her forehead that needed to be Botoxed out. Because Adam was attracted to Eve's essence, her body was to him a transparent window through which the contents could be seen. She was not all cover and no book. Rather, cover and book came together to make one sparkling package.

But then Adam and Eve sinned and lost their innocence. They ate from the tree of knowledge, subjective knowledge, the knowledge that comes from subjective experience. Like a man who thinks he can only know a woman by dating a great many, Adam now related to Eve through subjective comparison. Rather than looking at Eve and being innocently attracted to her, he could not help but compare her to subjective standards of beauty. Whereas before Adam asked himself, *Is Eve's body attractive to me?* he now questioned, *How does she compare to a supermodel? Is she tall compared to other women? She's a brunette, but maybe I'd be more attracted to a blonde.* Shallow things like size become important. Eve, feeling compared, became self-conscious, and her natural instinct was to cover up.

But Adam, too, was corrupted by the ingestion of subjective knowledge and became self-conscious about his own size, as so many men are today, both the size of their wallet as well as the size of their male appendage. The beauty of sex is the ability to just be. Sex allows us to proceed entirely on unpremeditated instinct. It has an innocence and a casualness to it that is the source of its pleasure. But now that Eve had also attained the knowledge born of experience, Adam felt compared to others and ran to protect himself and cover up.

Hence, after the sin Adam and Eve both have something to hide. It is their ugliness that they cover up. They became no different from the endless number of men and women today who are self-conscious about their bodies and feel permanently inadequate.

Dan and Mary came for counseling with an unfortunate story. After fifteen years of marriage, Dan had convinced his wife that the solution to the monotony of their monogamy was to start swinging. And because they would do it together, having sex with other couples rather than having secret affairs on their own, it would be something that would bring them closer. At first Dan had to push his wife to agree. She was uncomfortable showing her body to strange men, let alone having sex with them. But then, mostly out of the anger and hurt of watching her husband make out with other women, she decided to let go. She could not have predicted how much, after the initial discomfort, she would enjoy it. Feeling desirable to strange men made her feel youthful. But her pleasure in being with other men started to kill her husband. Whenever they would come home to their own bed and try to have sex, he would freeze up. He felt that every aspect of his masculinity was now being judged by his wife. His body wasn't as muscular as the men she was with. His organ wasn't as grand. His hands weren't as strong. His technique was not as developed. He felt that his wife was patronizing him when she told him he was a skilled lover. He became self-conscious and could not sustain an erection. After even Viagra failed to cure the problem, they came to see me. I explained to him that his tragic idea of bringing strangers into the innermost sanctum of their marriage had transformed the objective into the subjective. Before, Mary had looked at her husband and judged him by his objective and undeniable virtue. He was a loving man who was committed to her. He turned her on. Now, she looked at her husband, compared him to the other men she was with, and concluded that he was less manly than they were. At least that's how Dan perceived it. It took me many sessions to persuade Dan and Mary not only to reestablish the exclusivity of their union, but to purge themselves of the ghosts of lovers past and reestablish their innocence.

The loss of innocence manifested itself in a much different way with Nancy. Nancy, an attractive woman in her middle twenties, asked me if I could introduce her to a nice guy. I invited her to our home for the Friday night Sabbath meal where many young people usually join us, and she ended up meeting a friend of mine. After he took her out once, however, he would not do so again. I introduced her to another man, and he also took her out once but not a second time. Then the same thing happened with a third man. I couldn't understand why. On the surface she seemed like a great person. She was physically attractive, highly intelligent, with a promising career. So what was the problem?

I called her to see how she was doing. "Why do you ask?" she said, which sort of struck me as odd. After all, why was she being so defensive? "Well," I said carefully, "we're friends and it's polite for friends to ask how the other is doing." I then asked her how things were going at work. "They're fine. Why would you think there are any problems?" I then asked her some other seemingly benign questions, but each response was predicated with a variation of "Are you suggesting there's a problem?"

So that is the reason men aren't interested in her, I thought. *She is so defensive.* I couldn't even ask a simple question without her feeling attacked. Later, however, I realized that I was wrong. Men quickly lost interest in her not because of her defensiveness or paranoia. While those qualities may have irritated them, they wouldn't have diminished their attraction to her. Rather, they lost interest in her because they saw that she had lost her innocence. None of her responses came from the heart. They were all guarded and contrived.

I asked her why she had such a problem with trust. "All men have an agenda. They're interested in only one thing. They don't want to get to know you. They just want to use you." Okay, for some men that's probably true. But did she realize that this jaded attitude was a huge turnoff? It was almost as if she had made it her business to outsmart men, to show that she could be just as manipulative as they were. At some level, she was trying to be a man. And men just aren't as erotic as women. Feminine innocence is incredibly erotic because it invites a man to draw forth from that unstained fountain an explosive response. It is the ladylike, feminine woman that a man wishes to seduce so that he can release her dormant fire. But in the case of Nancy, obviously something had happened in her life that had robbed her of her innocence.

There is nothing so beautiful in life, or so attractive, as innocence. You can go to Disney World and be awed by the incredible "Magic Kingdom" that cost billions of dollars to build. You can go to New York City and be awestruck by the buildings that scrape the skies. And you can watch a *Star Wars*–variety sci-fi flick with the greatest technical effects. And yet this will never evoke the same majesty or awe as the Grand Canyon at sunset or the Grand Tetons in the shimmering sun. There is a purity to nature that can never be replicated by human ingenuity, however grand. There is a reason. Man-made objects are designed to impress, designed to overpower you. As such, they raise our defenses. We feel slightly manipulated into feeling small, so we subconsciously resist their effects. Since they raise our backs, they cannot carry us away with a feeling of awe-inspiring majesty. But the Columbia Glacier can. The Great Barrier Reef can. That's because natural things are not designed to *do* anything. They just are.

Similarly, a woman today can change every part of her face and body with plastic surgery. But the moment a man discovers that her breasts are made of silicon, he will not find her to be as attractive. When nature is manipulated it loses its innocence.

What makes the innocent person so deeply charming and erotic is the openness of their heart. Because their souls are translucent, you can see right through to their essence. Innocent people disarm us. Because they are so natural, they invite us to behave naturally around them as well, allowing for our deepest selves to be manifest. Indeed, they possess the unique gift of making us not have to take ourselves too seriously as they never invite competition. Similarly babies, the most innocent creatures of all, bring out the best in even the toughest people because they force us to be genuine. They cause us to stop acting and just "be ourselves." With babies we let down our guard, we make funny noises and faces in an effort to make them laugh. With adults, on the other hand, we mask our true selves with pretense because we seek approval and fear humiliation.

Unskilled in the art of manipulation, the innocent person accepts the humanity and infinite worth of every individual. With no agenda other than sharing, openness, and love, the innocent person allows us to lessen our guard as well. The manipulative person, on the contrary, sees others as the means by which to achieve his own selfish ends. He therefore causes the person he is interacting with to raise their defenses and be on the alert. Because he robs others of their innocence, however, the manipulator compromises not only his innocence but his humanity as well.

Innocence is about living honestly, not pretending to be that which we are not; not pretending to be happy or grieved when we are not. It is to be transparent in every situation and act honestly and genuinely. Indeed, this is perhaps the greatest problem that couples today suffer from—because they are not honest with themselves, they find it hard to be honest with others. And when we live in a world of such chicanery and masquerade, it becomes hard to trust, and the cycle perpetuates itself.

Sara and Patrick came to see me on the brink of divorce. Her complaint: Patrick is never home. He is always out with his friends. He has no need for me. His complaint: Sara is angry and aggressive. Of course I don't want to be around her. She's not pleasant. She's always pressuring me to be at home. Marriage has become like a cage. And my nature is that, whenever I feel pressure, I withdraw. After speaking with both of them for quite a while, it became clear that Sara was right. Patrick found excuses to be out of the home. Good excuses, but excuses nonetheless. He simply had no enjoyment for the domestic life. He enjoyed golfing with his buddies and traveling with them to exotic destinations. But the way Sara responded to his rejection just made the situation so much worse. She would write him angry e-mails: "Don't come home. Stay with your friends." I said to her, "Here is the problem, Sara. Your husband is definitely in the wrong. He devastates you by making you feel that he doesn't want to be with you. But then, instead of attacking him, why are you afraid to be honest? Tell him you want him home because you love him, because you need him. Tell him that when he's not with you, you're lonely. You desire him." But Sara could not be that open. Too many men had hurt her and she was no longer innocent. From the father who left the family when she was twelve, to the boyfriend who cheated on her in college, Sara had learned to not depend on men because they were not dependable. Although she had been hurt, and although her husband was at fault for not being a good husband, Sara still compromised her attractiveness by losing her innocence. And innocence is something that we should never allow to be taken away.

One of the best ways to recapture marital innocence, and therefore erotic desire, is for husbands and wives to learn to tell each other what they really desire from the relationship. You have to stop fearing need. Tell each other that you need each other. Reveal to one another your deepest needs, from emotional to sexual needs and everything in between. Most wives are too shy to open up to their husbands about what they really desire sexually. They're often embarrassed. What if it sounds weird or dirty? And husbands are usually not much better. What if my wife thinks that what I want is perverted or sick? But short of asking a third party to join your love-making sessions or becoming addicted to porn, there is nothing sick about your erotic desire, so long as it is used to bring the two of you closer. Emotional openness is the gate to innocence. You have to overcome the fear of baring your soul, or for that matter, exposing your raw desire. It's good to want one another—in every possible way.

The more we lose our innocence, the less emotional we are and the more intellectual we become. We begin to evaluate matters of love with our minds and rely less on the heart. Take a man and a woman who start dating. She lets her emotions go and allows herself to fall in love with him. They go to bed, and she never hears from him again. The next time she dates a guy, she will be on her guard and not allow herself to fall. In her eyes, he is going to try to get something off of her, so she is going to try to outsmart him. Because she will not trust him naturally, he will have to prove his love to her.

When we lose our innocence, our emotions always suffer the most. Emotions are meant to be automatic and intuitive, never contrived. They are all about letting go and allowing ourselves to feel and connect. And since this is so, whenever we are immersed in an environment where there is no trust, we train ourselves not to feel.

We can all become innocent again. We can all erase both the scars and the sins of our past. Take Angela, a listener to my radio show, who wrote to me that she was in a relatively new relationship with a good man whom she was developing strong feelings for. But she also had major trust issues. Her ex-husband had been unfaithful. Other relationships that had preceded her marriage had similarly caused pain. She wanted to know how she could disclose this to him without, first, judging him by their mistakes, or testing him to see if he would behave like these other men.

I wrote back to her that innocence is recaptured through intimate dialogue and fearless communication. Most people today, especially those who have been hurt, find it difficult to communicate. They are too inhibited, too afraid, too frightened of opening up. I told her that she must sit her boyfriend down and tell him that she wanted to share something important with him. That she loved him and cared for him. But in the past, a man she had loved had shattered her to the core by cheating on her. As a result, she had major trust issues. She had to admit that she knew this was a scar and that she was trying to heal herself of it. Nevertheless, she wanted him to know, not because she suspected him of cheating, but rather, should he surmise that she seemed slightly closed, she wanted him to know why. She believed that all people have to transcend painful experiences in order to once again become whole, and she was committed to doing so. In the meantime, he should never translate her reticence as rejection.

Now, why would this communication help Angela recapture her innocence? Because beneath all the pain, there was a real woman struggling with her emotions, fighting to become whole. And what she did in this moment of truth was to remove all the scar tissue and bring her boyfriend into her innermost heart. And that's where her innocence lay.

The same ability to regain innocence is true even for women who are vastly sexually experienced but who wish to connect intimately with a new man they love without being haunted by the ghosts of lovers past.

Jessica wrote to me after she became engaged to Michael. She was in terrible anguish. She had gone through a promiscuous streak in her early twenties and had had sex with more than twenty men. She felt guilty, as if she was bringing something dirty into her new marriage. "I am not that woman anymore," she said, "and even so, I feel like I have to tell my fiancé about them before we get married, but I am afraid he will be disgusted by me and break our engagement." She signed her name, "Ashamed and Afraid."

I wrote back, "I understand how painful it must be to feel you have to conceal an essential part of your identity from someone you love so much. Clearly the whole purpose of being in a relationship is being able to be utterly vulnerable, open and naked, and by naked I mean not in the literal sense, but in the metaphorical one. To remove all of our defensive armor and to feel that we are accepted for who we are. In every area of life we are judged by our externalities, by what we do, by how we present ourselves, by the impact we make. It is only in a loving relationship that we are judged by a completely different criterion, namely, what we *are*. It is our *being* that is embraced and not just our doing. Hence, your feeling of anxiety of being in a relationship, and yet on the other hand feeling fearful of rejection—that if your character were truly known, you would not be loved by the man whom you love, and whose affection you seek—is very understandable. You are afraid that you have lost your innocence and can never reclaim it. And all the residue of your former lovers will follow you into your marriage.

"Nothing could be farther from the truth. We all make mistakes in life. We all do things that we regret. Wrestling with our humanity is the very stuff of living. In life, righteousness is defined not through perfection, but rather through struggle. It is our endeavor to try to do the right thing amid a predilection to do otherwise that makes us unique, not the fact that we always *choose* the right thing.

"The bad things that you did in the past, losing your innocence, agreeing to be intimate with men who may not have loved you, compromising your sense of intimacy and dignity—those things are all in the past. They are no longer who you are. When we repent of the bad things that we do and commit to acting differently, then they are erased and our innocence is restored. In Jewish teaching, when a person changes their ways they are not even allowed to be reminded of their former self because those former paths apply to someone else. They are no longer that person. You should therefore certainly *not* share with your boyfriend the fact that you have been with many men. It was not *you* who was with those men. Now that you truly regret those actions, have changed your ways, have committed to a better path, you have become a different woman. You have changed, you are new. You are innocent. To bring that up would be bringing up a stranger, a foreigner. And this is especially true because your convictions have changed."

Why is it that so many erotic jokes are about virgins and nuns? And why is it that most men are attracted to virgins and less attracted to, say, strippers or prostitutes? Because nothing is more seductive in a woman than her innocence. Indeed, a chaste woman is far more alluring than a promiscuous one because she still possesses her mystery. Notice that you'll never find a lonely-hearts ad that reads: *Successful businessman with yacht and private airplane seeks former prostitute for long-term relationship and possibly marriage.*

But why not? A successful prostitute should make the best wife. She has a terrific body and she is sexually astute. She is also street-smart and financially aware. She is a virtual library of sexual information and, as a wife, is sure to give you a good time. Moreover, if she is good enough to spend your money on, then why is she not good enough to marry? Men do not marry prostitutes because once a woman has lost her innocence, she has lost much of her allure. You may pay her for sex but usually when you need it anonymously, you want it without complications, or because nothing else is available. One of the great gifts that a woman gives a man is that she makes him feel masculine. When he pleases her he feels strong and capable. When he makes her lose control, when he brings her to the heights of erotic abandonment, he feels that he has caused her to be born anew. But if he can make no original imprint because she is just too experienced, he is denied this great pleasure. He cannot transform her from a woman into a sexual being. She was already there well before he came into the picture.

My friend Carla was interested in James, so I invited them both to our home for dinner. James was taken by Carla's maturity and the way she carried herself throughout the evening, so he invited her out to lunch. Their relationship blossomed. Then unexpectedly, Carla sent him some supposedly funny pornographic images by e-mail. Perhaps she felt insecure and did this to show him that she had a sense of humor. After receiving a cartoon image of Fred Flintstone masturbating, James called and told me that he could no longer see Carla in the same, dignified light.

You may read this and think how prudish I sound for trumpeting the virtuous woman. But let me be democratic in my advice: The same rule applies equally to men. Innocent men are incredibly desirable, whereas men who are manipulative are the least sexy of all. The guys who try to dazzle women with their name-dropping and large bank accounts are kind of pathetic. Their actions betray a fear that there is nothing special about them. It's the soft, openhearted guys, the tortured souls who are unafraid to show their rawness, that women really want to rescue.

A number of years ago, while I was serving as rabbi at Oxford University, Roseanne Barr invited me on her television talk show to act as matchmaker to her three daughters. I carefully selected three special young men who would do me proud and please Roseanne and her very fine daughters. The first two were perfect on paper. Both were Oxford scholars. One was a former officer in the Israeli army pursuing a

doctorate in international relations. The other was the cap-
tain of the Oxford water polo team who was studying for a
degree in advance molecular engineering. The third bachelor
was more ordinary on paper. He had attended a regular college and was now working as a caterer in London. He balked
at my request. "I appreciate your faith in me, Shmuley, but I
don't really want to go. I'll feel intimidated. People will hear
about these great guys and then they'll compare me and I'll
look like a jerk."

But I knew that he was wrong. In fact, he had the one
quality that great Oxford scholars sometimes lack: he didn't
take himself too seriously. He was thoughtful and malleable,
a decent guy who treated everybody with respect. He had an
easy charm about him and was always prepared to laugh at
himself. "You're so wrong," I told him. "You're going to be
the most successful of all."

Sure enough, as soon as we brought the three of them on
the set, Roseanne turned to me during a commercial break
and said, "I like the caterer." Of the three attempted matches,
the caterer's was the only one that, at least for a while, worked
out. The reason for this was his innocence. He had no airs
about him, he was simply himself, and when you are simply
yourself you exude confidence. Think about it, when you
are simply yourself you have nothing to hide. You always live
honestly, never pretending to be that which you are not. It
is no coincidence that in survey after survey, women consistently rate confidence and humor as men's two most attractive qualities. Both are the products of innocence. Men also
can compromise their mystery by being manipulative and

insincere. Women today are especially weary of "professional romancers," men trained in the art of getting a woman to submit without any reciprocal desire to attach or commit.

The more important aspect of innocence is that it gives us the ability to be completely transformed through sex. Erotic virginity is our capacity to go from the mundane and non-sexual to the supremely sexual; it is innocence that allows this to happen. Men don't marry prostitutes because those women are unable to go through this transformation. Since the prostitute's sexuality is overt, she is unable to be transformed. She can't go from being a woman of mystery and modesty to a voracious sexual dominatrix. Because she begins as the latter, her eroticism is of limited bandwidth. No man can stoke her sexual fire since it's already burning at a high pitch from the moment you walk in the room. She is a woman ready for sex, not because you've aroused her but because it's what she does. She involves her body in the sexual act, but not her soul. Consequently, although she can offer a certain level of gratification, she can never provide the precious feeling of desirability to her clientele. Because her love is for hire, the passion she generates is never natural, always contrived, and always insincere. A man will never be satisfied with this kind of sexual union.

Furthermore, to employ the metaphor of the Jewish mystics, a woman's sexuality is like the coal hidden in a fire. If you ever light a barbeque, you know that inside the coals are burning hot embers. This internal fire lasts far longer than the flames that erupt at the surface, specifically because it is hidden. It is the kind of fire that burns without consuming. And like the fire that burns within the coals, a woman's sexuality, so much more potent than a male's, must be fanned into a flame in order to be made manifest. That is the purpose of foreplay.

In sex, men are like a triangle. They become instantly interested, like a steep-inclined plane, but immediately after achieving satisfaction they lose all interest. The same is not true of women, who resemble an arc in sex. It may take them a bit longer to get interested in the sexual endeavor, but once interested, they remain interested.

And this is the beautiful gift that a woman gives a man. She allows him to corroborate his masculinity by the extent to which he can make her femininity manifest. She gives him the unique key that can unlock her sexuality. Because a man not only wants to feel desired by a woman, he wants to know that he transforms her from a woman who is in control to a woman who submits to her passions and instincts. In the words of the old Carole King song, he wants to be responsible for making her "feel like a natural woman."

Sex can't work its magic without innocence because through innocence we allow ourselves to fully let go and be embraced by the overwhelming power of the sexual experience. A man makes a woman feel desirable, a woman makes a man feel masculine from the desire he creates in her. But if both parties have come to the bed with no ability to give these gifts to one another, then sex will always be an empty exercise. The ability to experience the transformation from nonsexual to sexual is highly erotic. And innocence is a state of being that allows us to participate in this mental journey between perception and actuality.

Some advice for married women to cultivate their innocence is this. Never walk around the bedroom naked. Dress modestly even in the privacy of your home. Make your husband earn every view of your body. At times give him glimpses, but only for a moment or two. If he wants a prolonged peek, better for him to see you when you are both in an aroused state. Don't take showers in front of him, and please, don't ever go to the bathroom in front of him. Same applies to flossing your teeth. There are areas of marriage where we are to preserve our innocence, preserve our privacy, and cultivate mystery.

Few things have been as injurious to the modern marriage as the mistaken belief that in marriage you are meant to be open about everything. Bullocks. Good marriages have zones of privacy. Don't take care of your hygienic requirements in front of each other.

Furthermore, don't bring up past loves to your spouse. With the sole exception of a husband sometimes giving his wife an erotic interrogation and questioning her about her previous love affairs with the intention of exploring her sexual mind, previous relationships have no place in your marriage. And for men, this is an absolute rule. Aside from the most practical considerations, do not discuss your previous girlfriends with your wife, even when she wants to talk about it. She is bound to feel that you are comparing her in some way. And don't think about them either, especially when you are making love to your wife.

Because innocence also means the manifestation of your truest self, including your sexual self, once a week husbands and wives should have erotic conversations about their deepest sexual desires. Often the best time to conduct these conversations is in the car when you are both alone. You're both sitting forward, and avoiding eye contact is initially helpful in dealing with the natural shyness that such a conversation engenders. And you have to struggle through the initial discomfort. Otherwise, you become one of those tragic couples who never truly know each other. You didn't get married to have half a soul mate.

And finally, after these conversations become a bit more comfortable, you can practice one of the most erotically innocent techniques of all: developing nonverbal communication. At first, we express our innermost desires verbally. The conversation is a bit awkward. Gradually, it becomes more comfortable and then more intimate. But the strongest passions cannot be limited to words. So you sit together, sometimes naked, sometimes clothed. Your faces are pressed up close to each other. It's silent all round. And then you stare right directly into each other's eyes. You keep the gaze focused for at least ten minutes. You try not to look away. And then, it happens. You begin to communicate your deep desire to your spouse directly through the medium of the eyes, the window to the soul. You feel a deeper, more intimate connection than your marriage has ever had. And to make the exercise even more compelling, you sometimes break the spell by asking your spouse to guess what it was you were telling them. It's an explosive and powerful exercise. You'll be bewitched!

But eroticism doesn't thrive on innocence alone. There are, in fact, seven other secrets by which eroticism lives. Let's move on.

THE SECOND
SECRET:
NOVELTY

Love is what happens to men and women
who don't know each other.
—W. SOMERSET MAUGHAM

It doesn't take a genius to know that one of the leading reasons men cheat on their wives is for the sake of being with someone new. Men crave variety.

It's true, newness is erotic. The thought of a new experience, a new lover, a new body, the way we see ourselves again through someone else's eyes—all of that is exciting and attractive. Remember your first love, when you felt dazed and ecstatic? Novelty shakes things up. There is a new and intense vibration. Novelty is an essential ingredient in eroticism. The problem is that it wanes in marriage.

When there is no novelty, there comes a vicious downward spiral. A couple falls into routine. Sex dwindles. Men become bored with their wives, and they withdraw their sexual energy from their relationships. The wives respond by feeling neglected and therefore bitter. Their bitterness then leads the husband to feel justified in transferring their erotic attention on to other women. Maybe they'll go after the cute new secretary at work. Their wives feel their husband's lack of interest, which propels them not to want to have sex with them, which in turn pushes their husbands further away, perhaps into the arms of someone else who gives them some attention. Their wives feel asexual and unattractive, and try to fill the void with things that won't actually fill it, like an addiction to shopping and spending money.

The reason this happens is that men fail to realize that their own wives have deep sexual reservoirs. Like diving into the ocean and discovering a beautiful coral reef, if a man just penetrated his wife's erotic mind he would discover a world of color and vibrancy. He would find a wife with vivid sexual fantasy, a wife who is wholly attuned to the attraction that men have for her and who cannot help but feeling pangs of attraction to them in turn. A wife who perhaps even pleasures herself to the thought of those other men. In many ways, she cannot help it. Women are much more sexual than men. Their sexuality strikes much more deeply than men. It is not divorced from the emotions as it often is with men. A woman's sexual needs are much more pronounced, if not as revealed, than a man's. Unfortunately, however, the average husband is not a scuba diver but a snorkeler. He penetrates a few inches deep, employs the same sexual position over and over again, has quickie sex with her, and then wonders why both of them are so bored. These are the men who are don't believe that their wives fantasize. Many don't believe that their wives are really interested in sex at all.

Keith and Najlah were married four years with a deteriorating sex life that had diminished to about once a month.

Keith complained that no matter what he tried, Najlah could not and would not climax. He would stimulate her in every which way, all in vain. She would lie there limp and unengaged. They both agreed that in all the years they had been married she had not climaxed even once. When they were together, Keith began to feel emasculated. He got depressed. What made it worse was the way Najlah confessed to him that she had started, only recently, to stimulate herself when he wasn't around. When she was alone her body worked. But not with Keith, no matter how patient he was with her.

In counseling it emerged that it wasn't Najlah who was bored with Keith, but quite the reverse. Outside the bedroom, Keith utterly ignored Najlah. He didn't call her during the day and he didn't speak to her at night. He lived instead for two passions: making money and following sports. He told me, "I like making money because it's challenging and it earns people's respect. Football lets me blow off steam and relax." "And your wife?" I asked him. "Yeah, she's okay. Not the most exciting person. But I do love her." No wonder Najlah couldn't respond to his touch. She felt like yesterday's newspaper being put to a new use, like wiping up a coffee stain. Keith needed to make his wife climax in order to wipe away his shame. But he had no real interest in her as a woman, and she felt it. I advised him not to be intimidated by the fact that his wife was seeking sexual pleasure herself, but to explore it. "After all of these dead ends, this is a portal into your wife's erotic mind. This will finally give you the novelty you need to see her as much more interesting than one of your stock deals." But Keith couldn't do it. He felt ineffectual and intimidated. He felt his wife didn't need him. Little did he realize that he had initiated the cycle of rejection.

Feminine sexuality is the real secret of novelty in marriage. Unlike men, who are usually content to go through the same sexual motions and focus simply on achieving climax, a woman's sexuality is infinitely varied and constantly renewing itself. Unlike a man's, a woman's libido is emotional rather than pornographic, interested in erotic stories rather than dirty pictures. A husband who sees his wife as an infinite riddle is mentally engaged for long intervals. Female sexuality is a mystery of great complexity. Its secret is captured in the female genitalia themselves, which, unlike the jutting and exposed male genitals that are anything but complex, are hidden, covered, and consist of fold after fold. A husband is given the opportunity to metaphorically peel back each fold and expose fresh layers of erotic interest. That's the secret of sexual novelty in marriage.

Sadly, so few husbands take their wives' sexual complexity seriously. They view their wives as being sexually monolithic. They reduce them to skin and body parts, and quickly get bored. Most husbands go through life only scratching the surface of their wives' hidden sexual reservoir. Ironically, it's usually a lover—to whom she is forbidden and new—who will plumb its depths and discover it.

I had known Jeffrey my entire life. One day he came to me to confess that he was having an affair. I asked him why he was doing this to his wife. "My wife simply doesn't attract me anymore. She undresses and I can barely bring myself to look. I'm just not interested in her anymore." I gave him the following advice. "Tonight, I want you to drive with your wife to the next town. Go into a loud and raunchy bar but go in separately. No one should know you're together. She has to sit by the bar and you, like a fly on the wall, will just watch." "Then what?" Jeffrey asked me. "You'll see for yourself."

It took some cajoling, but Jeffrey and his wife agreed to the strange advice. When they arrived at the club, Jeffrey's wife walked in alone and sat by the bar. Jeffrey came in half an hour later. One man had sat down right next to his wife and was trying to buy her a drink. The bartender was flirting with her. Another man was angling to sit next to her on the other stool. Jeffrey was incensed. He was beside himself with jealousy. He broke the rule of not letting on that they were together, grabbed his wife by the hand, told the men she was married, and pulled her outside. In the parking lot, he yelled at her that she was a slut, pulled her into the car, and made the most passionate love to her that he had in years. It was the novelty of discovering the sexual depths of a wife he scarcely knew existed that fired Jeffrey's erotic passion for his wife anew.

On my radio show I once hosted a bad-boy author who had written a book about how he could seduce any woman in the world. In the middle of the interview he issued a brazen warming to the listeners: "To all you investment bankers, all you doctors, all you lawyers out there. I earn a fraction of what you earn. I drive an old jalopy. But I could get any one of your wives. I could steal them away from you in just a few days. I know what she wants in ways that you could never understand. Be warned. Beware." It was an arrogant boast, and I scolded him for his hubris. "I'm not arrogant," he said, defending himself. "It's not about arrogance. I could steal away their wives not because I'm a better man or a better lover, but because these guys don't appreciate their wives. They don't want to know them. But I do. I could get their wives not by flexing my muscles or showing off my six-pack. I could get them simply by listening to them. I really listen to women. I think they have something to say. I find them endlessly fascinating. And what I've discovered is that the average husband doesn't believe that. They're bored with their wives and they chase other women instead. But I never get bored of a woman." Now, granted, I took everything he said with a big pinch of salt. After all, if he was this great appreciator of women, why wasn't he with *one*? Why was he a womanizer? But still he had a very good point. Men turn to buying cars, boats, and following sports for excitement. And in the process they neglect their soul mates and families.

On *Shalom in the Home* we worked with a couple who hadn't had sex in more than a year. The husband said it was his wife who had lost interest, this just after they had had another baby. I assured him that was balderdash. We arranged an activity to jump-start their love interest. I told his wife that she was going to be our guest at a fancy spa where she would be pampered. She would also have a massage. She was introduced to the sexy young masseur. Little did she realize that we were going to switch him for her own husband after the lights went out. The masseur stayed in so his voice would mislead her, but the actual massage was given by her husband. I told him before it started to go for the gold. "Go to places where a legitimate masseur would never go. I bet she'll let you." Sure enough, she basically did. He couldn't believe it. As he really began to push it, she lifted her head and discovered it had been her husband all along. But no matter. His passion for his wife had been reawakened. The woman who had no interest in sex, to his mind, had now become one lusty lady. All along his wife had been that lady, but he had never seen it. All I had done in this admittedly brazen exercise was to show him his wife in a totally new light. And it was the novelty that lit the erotic fire in his ... uh ... hands. But he could easily have found the same novelty himself and lit the fire himself.

Domesticity is the downfall of novelty. Uninspired marriages almost always kill off eroticism. Routine kills eroticism. And the mental perception that we are in an "'old" relationship likewise snuffs out the spark. In truth, there is no such thing as an old relationship. We do not get married at the altar once and for all. On the contrary, we have to renew our commitment to our partner every single day.

I got married at twenty-one in Sydney, Australia. The day after the wedding I walked to a shopping mall to buy a camera to take pictures of me and my new bride. I felt totally in love and absolutely excited by my new wife. I was horrified, therefore, to notice that the woman who sold me the camera was attractive. What? You mean I could notice another woman's attractiveness even after getting married? I came home and confessed my terrible sin to my wife, who just laughed. But it bothered me and I spent time pondering why love is so imperfect. Later, I understood that the innocent attraction to strangers had its merits because G-d wanted me to choose my bride anew every single day. Had I never been attracted to anyone else, the marriage would have grown moldy and old. But the fact that we are attracted to strangers means that we have to reaffirm our commitment to our spouse on a daily, even hourly basis. Our love can never grow stale. Our spouse is being constantly chosen, thereby validating their uniqueness.

In order to reignite eroticism, married couples need to occasionally do crazy, out-of-the-box things that bring out novelty. Have sex with the blinds open with the possibility that someone might see. Have sex in the back of the family minivan. Okay, forget the minivan. You'll hurt yourselves against the children's lunchboxes. Rent a snazzy convertible and do it with the the roof down. Have sex while one or the other is having a normal conversation on the phone and is forced to conceal what is going on. Your wife is speaking to the landscaper about the new flower bed he has to install. Start nuzzling her ear. She'll push you away. Don't give up. Soon, she'll begin to respond. But she'll have to mute her reaction while the phone call is on. Ah, but this stuff is crazy. You might get caught. That's the whole point. Push the envelope. Do new things you would never otherwise do. Think in novel ways. You need newness and you cannot allow your marriage to atrophy.

Eroticism can also be found in the novelty of having conversations on subjects you would otherwise never discuss. Whether it's your darkest sexual fantasy, or something utterly unrelated to sex, like your darkest emotions or fears, simply going to a place that the two of you have never gone to before is enough to jump-start novelty. So go beyond your comfort zone. Talk about things you're reluctant to discuss. Turn yourself inside out. Invert yourself and let the seams show. It will kindle the fire of erotic passion.

Like we saw before with Jeffrey and his wife's bar experiment, novelty can also be achieved by husbands looking at their wives through other men's eyes. Sometimes this comes about, tragically, when it's too late. As a marriage counselor I have discovered that simply reminding a man how special his wife is or reminding a woman of how fortunate she was in her choice of husband is enough to restore appreciation and passion in a relationship. Too often it comes about only when it's too late.

This was the circumstance of Mel, a man who came to see me because he had discovered that his wife was having four-hour phone calls with a stranger. He confronted her and she confessed that she was in a relationship with a man she met on a plane. He sank into a deep depression. When the two came to see me, he was yelling at his wife even as they sat down in my living room. It was painful to watch. He blamed himself for losing his wife. He said he had a problem showing affection, that he loved his wife but didn't know how to express it. It was only now that he had pushed her into another man's arms that he realized just how deeply he loved her. And the saddest thing about this session was that he had alienated his wife so thoroughly that even as she watched him disintegrate before both of our eyes, she never changed her stone-cold expression. The most we could get from her was, "Mel, I'm sorry that I hurt you."

The benefits of seeing your wife through the eyes of another man need not come about in such tragic circumstances. I often tell husbands and wives to walk together on a beach, walk together down the street, with the husband walking a few steps behind. He sees all the men looking at an attractive woman walking on her own. He is *reminded* that his wife is not just the mother of his children, but first and foremost a woman. Husbands usually make the mistake of thinking that novelty can only come in the form of staring at bodies of new women, which is why they are so often sexually distracted in marriage. In truth, novelty comes not from seeing new women, but from seeing new men stare at the same woman, your wife. What you require is not a new body, but a new set of eyes.

Husbands: Coax a sexual fantasy out of your wife. Discovery is a huge part of eroticism and discovery precipitates novelty. Put yourself in a situation where you can see that other men are attracted to your wife, whether it's her sitting alone for a few minutes at a bar or watching her as she works out in a gym. And always beware of the male trainer, to whom so many women open up. The male trainer is the new hairdresser, only he's heterosexual and oh so interested. And interesting. Maybe you should be the male trainer. Start working out with your wife. Watch her as she contorts her body into new positions that you did not think possible. It will kindle erotic lust.

Novelty has two dimensions. There is actual newness—physical newness. Then there is perceptual newness—the act of delving into the deep and creating new awareness. And perceptual newness creates physical novelty, because new dimensions actually do come out. Superficial novelty can be like cocaine for sexual boredom. It gives us the jolt we are looking for, but it is ephemeral. When novelty becomes an extension of the mind's desire to seek higher plateaus, then it can be useful in energizing a boring sex life. The second kind of novelty requires us to change our thought patterns. It is finding newness where none seems to exist.

We look for novelty in the wrong places. We look for it in physical objects, in new lovers, and the like. But these do not sustain eroticism. Furthermore, when we go from thing to thing we can never develop the emotional depth that is needed to sustain genuine eroticism. When you approach eroticism in the first sense of novelty, the newness dissipates, and you are left with nothing because you have not invested any mental energy. If there is no mental energy, there is no eroticism.

The Bible advocates that novelty comes about through sexual distance, a monthly period of sexual abstinence lasting approximately twelve days. The Jewish faith calls this "the laws of family purity." It mandates that for the five days of menstruation and seven days thereafter, a couple physically separate, sleeping in separate beds, refraining from physical contact, and not seeing each other's naked bodies. When the separation period is over, the reunion is electrifying and climactic. The sexual rejoining is pure, novel, and erotically charged. Notice how some of the best sex in marriage is had, paradoxically, after an argument. The emotional distance created by the quarrel makes you feel new to each other when the argument is over. That's why makeup sex is so popular, even if it is usually unhelpful in solving the argument.

Now fighting, obviously, isn't the answer. We don't need to verbally abuse each other in marriage in order to discover latent passion. A monthly period of sexual separation is even more effective. It makes a man's wife sinful and forbidden to him. And sinfulness is yet another ingredient in eroticism that we'll shortly explore. It makes your bodies brand new to each other. There's also an intellectual aspect to this. Sometimes a conversation that doesn't deal with routine activities, or kids, or basic things is exactly what the doctor ordered. When you can find out what your spouse feels about bigger things, they reveal themselves a little more. Put your spouse outside of an "everyday life" context.

If we learn to cultivate the trait of perceiving things in a new way, our lives take on new dimensions and serve as great mysteries to unravel. You can use this to bring joy into other aspects of your life, when you realize your mind is capable of making anything new.

THE THIRD
SECRET:
THE CHASE

The important thing is not to stop questioning.
Curiosity has its own reason for existing.
—ALBERT EINSTEIN

It's true that we yearn for what we don't have and we grow weary of what we do have, and this is why The Chase, or the necessity of putting up obstacles between you and the object of your desire, is the third secret of eroticism. People always seem to strive for that which lies just outside their reach. This would seem to explain why obstacles that frustrate the fulfillment of our sexual desire are so fundamental to erotic lust. But this alone is an inadequate understanding of why erotic obstacles are so important. It actually goes well beyond a simple impediment to sexual attainment. Rather, what erotic obstacles provide is a substantiation of our desirability—*that someone will work to overcome every impediment to have us.* And that makes us feel incredibly sexy and desirable.

For a man or a woman to *feel* desirable, to feel erotic, they have to exude an overpowering force that is irresistible to the opposite sex. Submission is only meaningful where there are hurdles to its actualization.

Only a woman can validate a man's masculinity because only a woman can make a man feel erotically desirable. It's when she desires him as a man and cannot resist his masculine pull that his desirability as a man is validated. She feels the pull, he feels erotic. If she just gives herself to him without a struggle, then his masculinity is not established. She didn't submit because he was irresistible; she did it for external considerations. He gets her, but he doesn't feel masculine or wanted. If she submits because she can't help it, that's when he can fully experience his attractiveness.

Likewise, from a woman's standpoint, when she puts obstacles in front of a man that he is forced to surmount, it reveals the degree of his lust for her. That's why modest clothing is such an erotic turn-on. The body is concealed behind all manner of barriers that must be removed before she can be had. He will jump through all kinds of hoops to have her.

About two years ago my daughter came to me and complained about the paucity of modest clothing available in department stores for religious girls. The clothing that did exist that covered you up was frumpy, ugly, and uninspiring. From there was born my daughter's idea to one day create a clothing line of modest wardrobe that was colorful, form-fitting, and striking. My contribution to her idea was the tag line: modest is the new sexy.

Indeed it is. Attraction is created by that which is hidden, by that which is concealed, by that to which there are obstacles to its attainment. Is anyone really interested in seeing Britney's private parts after they were splashed all over the Internet? Or does the whole thing become not just tasteless but gross? Ironically, Britney removing her underwear made her less, not more, sexy. Pamela Anderson flashed her mammaries for a decade. Anyone still looking?

While eroticism is manifest in the body, it is created in and sustained by the mind. That's why pornographic forms of eroticism leave us feeling empty. There are no obstacles. They are purely material and leave no room for the individual soul to discover its own intricacy. Ironically, eroticism must be built on obstacles that subvert its fulfillment. Nothing is erotic unless its attainment is constantly frustrated. There must be something that gets in the way. It must be built on things that require leaping over its obstructions. That's why the woman with a brain will always be more deeply alluring than the woman with merely a bust. Her mind subverts a man's erotic pursuit. She can outmaneuver him and is never easily manipulated. He works to master her. But she is wily and always outflanks him. And the hunt goes on.

Whereas some of my Islamic brothers and sisters see the purpose of modesty as preventing men from having bad thoughts, Judaism insists that we cover the body for precisely the opposite effect. Men and women dress modestly in order to enhance the natural attraction of the masculine and feminine poles, so that when they marry and become intimate the act of removing clothing will elicit powerfully erotic thoughts and actions. The human body will never lose its magnetism because of the obstacles that frustrate its revelation.

Here's the truth of the matter. Modest women are the sexiest of all. They look feminine, desirable, and their covered bodies invite male curiosity. True, they might not get the immediate stare of the exposed cleavage. But the difference is that the man will stay focused on the covered woman's flesh well after her cleavage-bearing sister has nothing left to offer. The modest woman who conceals her sexuality invites a man to reveal it, always teasing the possibility of more. And what is eroticism if not the arousal of limitless possibility?

The modestly dressed woman, with her sleeves, stockings, and long-flowing skirt, is not just a model of femininity but is super-desirable to boot. Her modest reserve is erotically irresistible. These are girls who do not date recreationally. They are no man's game and are thus absent of artifice and guile. Their innocence invites further erotic interest. They do not dress in a manner that would manipulate. They do not use flirtation to slip under a man's armor. Less so do they use their sexuality to gain power. Rather, they exude an openness that draws forth a man's emotional nakedness. And by giving a man a safe arena within which to express his feelings and overcome his fears, he comes to not just love a woman, but to respect and be stimulated by her. Because encased in that attractive body is an even more attractive mind.

Eroticism invites the mind to be invested in the sexual experience. It is the fusion of the material and the spiritual, the body with the soul. And if we approach eroticism as a quest to unearth the great mystery of existence, then this develops into a wellspring of fulfillment and passion, a wellspring that will never run dry.

It is the mind, rather than our genitals, that are our principal sexual organ. In the mind lies the realm of fantasy. The more the mind participates in the sexual, the stronger the erotic becomes. That's why intelligence is an aphrodisiac.

Did I say intelligence? Yes, brains are sexy. Just ask any of those superhot professors at universities where everyone seems to have a crush on them. Eroticism is fostered by intelligent conversation. Meeting people who know is a turn-on. Meeting someone vastly knowledgeable and insightful is arousing because it invites the possibility that they will come to know you as well. Their knowledge is born of curiosity, and I said earlier, Eros is curiosity incarnate. It is a desire to peel back the layers and expose the essence.

Women love meeting smart, knowledgeable men. They find intellectuals erotic, which is why Marilyn Monroe will marry a great playwright like Arthur Miller and is also why Albert Einstein's biographers reveal the many women he had in his life.

Married couples often lose the erotic spark because they lose their intellectual edge. They let their brains get lazy. Rather than reading edifying books, they read the tabloids in bed. Rather than having interesting conversations over dinner about the state of the world or the meaning of life, they will talk about the neighbors. But a deep and insightful conversation that engages the mind is the earliest stage of foreplay. It really is.

Men know this. Men who are world-class seducers will take a woman on a date and they will begin to wax poetic about life and its challenges. They will invite a woman into their soul as they scrutinize their insecurities and flaws. By doing so, they not only portray themselves as vulnerable, but as thoughtful, inspired creatures who are sensitive to life. They may even quote poetry or some great philosopher. And they can feel the woman getting weak at the knees. It's *so* erotic.

So why don't husbands do this with their wives? I love history. And I always try to share with my wife interesting facts about historical personalities as I read them in biographies. I will try to understand the enigma of Abraham Lincoln and share with my wife my solution for solving the great man's riddle. In so doing, I not only connect with my wife on an intellectual level, but truth be told, I believe she becomes more attracted to me. I am a man with a smattering of depth.

Tom's wife was going to leave him, although they had two kids, because he was smoking marijuana every night. They had not had sex in six months. Tom tried; his wife pushed him away. She told him repeatedly that she was no longer in love with him. "Get this, Tom," I told him. "It's simply not sexy for a woman to make love to a dim-witted pothead. You've turned your brain into mush. Get off this stuff and start using your mind. Is this what you really are? An empty-headed Neanderthal who lives on weed? Throw the garbage out and do this. Start reading aloud to your wife every night. Choose the great classics, a great biography, a famous poem. Find an idea a day that you find scintillating and tell your wife why the idea interests you." Miracles do happen, and Tom, who was always a deep, albeit depressed soul, began to listen to me. He read the dark poetry of Edgar Allen Poe to his wife at night and would then tell her what he thought of what he had read. It was a turn-on and aroused his wife's erotic interest in him again. They started making love after both their libidos nearly died. Because the libido, just like the mind, is a terrible thing to waste.

Erotic obstacles build up tension, delay gratification, and increase the power of sex. The allure of obstacles is the opportunity to submit to our deepest desires. This is what is erotic about barriers. They provide potential to transfer from one state to another.

Some other ideas for erotic obstacles: Make out with your clothes *on*. Yes, on. Leave them on. At least for the first hour. *Did he say an hour? But usually sex lasts only seven minutes.* True, that's because you're both naked and you run straight to the finish line. But if you leave your clothing on, kissing, foreplay will be prolonged. Your mutual unavailability will stoke the fieriest of passions. Arousal will be enhanced.

Another idea. When you are geographically separated, have long erotic phone conversations. The fact that you are unavailable to one another frustrates consummation and increases desire. Too many couples miss out on the opportunity to enhance their relationship by having erotically charged conversations when they are physically unavailable to one another.

Yet another: Join the kosher sex club. Initiate a period of sexual separation in your marriage. Every two weeks, separate sexually for a few days. Limit other physical contact as well. Let your libido replenish itself. Sleep in pajamas so that your naked bodies don't touch. Talk in bed rather than touch each other. The conversations will heighten desire. If you can make it to twelve days, the biblical mandate, all the better. On the night of your reunion, make it into an event.

In Jewish circles, the wife immerses herself in a ritual bath. She pampers herself and dresses up for her erotic reunion with her husband. But the onus is not only on the wife to be a seductress. He should go to a store and buy her sexy lingerie. Becoming a gentleman who buys flowers and champagne is a nice touch. Although by now you'll be panting for one another, do things slowly. A great big erotic obstacle—physical separation—has been imposed in your relationship. Your lust has been jump-started. Dismantle the barrier slowly. Mr. Gorbachev, tear down that wall. But only one brick at a time. Start by kissing. Then remove articles of clothing slowly, one by one. Give each other long, sensual massages. Wait, slow down, fellah. She's not going anywhere. She's just getting started. Every move should involve an obstacle. Don't go straight to the usual erogenous zones. Go first to the ears, the hair, the elbows, and the knees. Now it's time to move more inwardly. You get the picture. And if you finish your reunion night in anything under ninety minutes, you've done things way too fast. Repeat from the beginning.

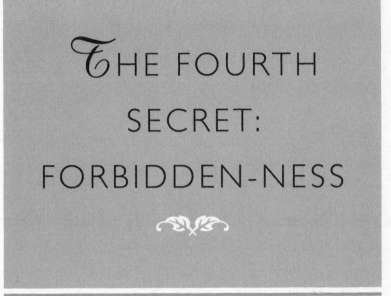

THE FOURTH
SECRET:
FORBIDDEN-NESS

Things forbidden have a secret charm.
—TACITUS

*A*ll you male readers (what? There are only two of you?), come with me for a brief mental journey. Close your eyes and imagine you're walking on a beach. You're surrounded by women in skimpy bikinis. They are all around you, practically naked. Is the place sexy? Hmmm, yeah. You bet. But is it erotic? Absolutely not. Here's proof. What do most men do at a beach? Either read a book, throw a Frisbee around, or fall asleep. So how erotic could the place be? So erotic that it put you to sleep? But then, that night you're walking your dog in your neighborhood, and a woman has accidentally left the blinds open in her bedroom. She is moving around in her bra and underwear. Is it sexy? Yup. Is it erotic? Are you kidding? Absolutely. Anyone planning to read a book or fall asleep? Hey, why not stop looking for a moment and pull out a Frisbee and invite some guy to throw it around with you. I don't think so, bud. But why not? What changed here? She is wearing the same amount of clothing as the bikinis at the beach. So why is the bedroom scenario so erotic where the beach was not? There's a difference. The women at the beach were wearing public attire. Okay, not much, but public nonetheless. So what you saw was what you were *supposed* to see. Because it was all so legal and expected, there was nothing erotic about it. But this woman is wearing something that is *not* supposed to be seen by anyone. You're seeing something you're not supposed to see. You're peering into her inner sanctum, witnessing her in her private attire. And she doesn't even know you're looking. You're being granted carte blanche access into a woman's private feminine world without her even being aware of it. This is sinful, forbidden, and deeply erotic. The same is true with anything sexual that is forbidden and sinful. It's always deeply erotic.

This presents a problem with marriage, which is, of course, all too legal. What destroys the eroticism of marriage is that it's so lawful. Sex with your wife? Not only are you allowed to, man, you're *supposed* to. Heck, you're *obligated* to. Which makes her body automatically nonerotic. There is nothing sinful about it. It doesn't push the boundaries, it doesn't break the rules. The same applies with seeing each other's naked bodies. Not only is it allowed, the conventional wisdom is that you should prance around the bedroom stark naked. There is never supposed to be any kind of inhibition about each other's bodies.

On my radio show, we once did a program about husbands and wives going to the bathroom in front of each other. I said it was a terrible thing that ought never to be done. But I was overruled by the vast majority of my female listeners who thought I was a Stone Age prude. Imagine, going to the bathroom in front of your wife, or in front of your husband. Uuugh! And people thought this was a good thing because it removed inhibition from marriage. Sure, go ahead and relieve yourself in front of your spouse. Break wind, eat your earwax. Heck, you're married. What could it hurt?

Only your erotic attraction to each other. That's all.

Yes, marriage is way too open, way too legal, way too available, which is why marriage requires a healthy dose of forbiddenness.

Going back to the Jewish tradition of the twelve-day separation, it works to create sinfulness in marriage—the good kind of sin. Your spouse becomes as prohibited to you as a stranger. The act of kissing or touching becomes sinful. They are off-limits by the highest power in the universe, G-d himself. And because the legal has been converted to the sinful, the seeds of eroticism have been planted. Suddenly, you're working to catch glimpses of your wife when she is in the shower. You're even looking at her undergarments that have been left around the bedroom. You're studying the black lacy bra she left outside the shower. Heck, before you didn't stare at them even when they were on her body. Now you're looking at them in her drawers. Before, when she was permitted to you, she would walk around the room naked and you would read the *Wall Street Journal*. Now, when she bends over fully clothed, you're sneaking glimpses of her cleavage. Cool. And hot. Imagine that. A man contorting his head to see his wife rather than his secretary's cleavage.

Others may not see it this way, but I have always believed
that the purpose of the twelve-day period of sexual abstinence mandated by the Bible is to have a husband do his dandiest to get his wife to submit within those twelve days—a
grave sin—and have his wife do her dandiest to fend him off.
Just the way two illicit lovers do. And just the way the two of
you probably did things before you were married, with him
pushing the limits and with you resisting as much as possible.
Yes, you're not supposed to submit. Nor should you. The laws
are serious. But the desire the effort engenders is downright
explosive, and when the appropriate times comes, twelve days
later, the force of your reunion is nuclear.

An article in the *New York Times* book section in June of
2008 detailed two books that came out at the same time
written by married couples who, in an effort to resurrect a
moribund sex life, agreed to have sex every night for about
one hundred days straight. The books made news because of
how tiresome that kind of frequency would be today, where
the national average is about once a week. Both couples reported that, after the sex marathon was over, they basically
suffered from sexual burnout and went about a month without having it.

When I read about these books I was amazed that they had
attracted any attention at all. Both were young and healthy
married couples. Was it really news that they had sex every
night? What couple wouldn't? You're both young and virile;
you sleep in the same bed; you're married for goodness' sake.
What should rather be making news are all those couples who
aren't having it! The Talmud, written two thousand years ago,

goes so far as to say that a man of leisure, that is, a man whose occupation does not involve strenuous exertion, is *obligated* to make love to his wife every single night. And that's because his wife wants it every night. The rabbis of the Talmud understood women to be much more sexual than men. And to the extent that today so many married women claim instead to have a headache is because their husbands are having such bad sex with them that they've killed off their libidos.

Marriage says that your sexual partner will only ever be your spouse. How then can marriage, predicated as it is on the exclusivity of a contract, ever enjoy the pleasures of sin and Eros? The answer is that life in general, and marriage in particular, must be made sinful. There has to be, strange as it sounds, an illegal aspect of life, a sinful aspect that breeds an erotic spark.

Judaism, with its extensive laws, introduces the concept of the forbidden into endless areas of life, even mundane acts like eating a meal. Judaism forbids us from simply devouring an animal. To do so is sinful. But there is a process that may be undertaken of slaughtering the beast, draining it of blood, preparing it according to traditional requirements. The animal is thereby rendered kosher. The transformation of the sinful into the permissible, of the forbidden into the acceptable, injects the simple act of eating with the pleasure of the erotic.

In fine dining establishments they take their time in serving you the food. Even if it were ready in an instant, they would still make you wait. Because they know that waiting for the food increases your appetite and heightens your desire.

Conversely, the fast-food restaurants are not only selling you food of a lower quality, they are also undermining your interest in the food by giving you instant gratification. You'll continue to buy from them because you're hungry. But you're always going to complain that the food is substandard.

In fine dining establishments they also dim the lighting, cultivating an air of mystery, while in fast -food joints they flood you in lighting, hoping you'll feel exposed, leave, and make room for the next customer.

There are many ways to bring sinfulness and the forbidden into your marriage. Try touching your wife's leg—or more— under the table on a double date with friends, and all along she will have to control and conceal the sensations you are awakening. You could make love on the side of the highway, risking being arrested by the police. Okay, I'm kidding. You don't have to bring the cops into this, but do push the envelope. Or, you could make an erotic video together that you would then have to put in a safe. All of this is healthy because sin is necessary. It's only when we sin that we often get to unleash our innermost self that so often becomes buried under stultifying layers of social propriety. And sin is where you throw caution to the wind. You can no longer be stifled. Your hunger, your lust, can no longer be suppressed. The beast within is awakened. But let it be awakened for and by your wife! Then it's healthy sin.

Another good exercise to bring forbidden-ness and sinfulness into marriage is to get your wife to reveal to you the petty attractions she has to other men. All wives have them. All wives deny them. All wives can slowly be coaxed to reveal them. These are sinful thoughts. Get her to talk about them.

On *Shalom in the Home* we had a husband who was hypercritical of his wife, always putting her down, finding fault with everything she did. I was counseling the two of them on a couch. The wife was beautiful but looked utterly beaten down, tired, distraught. I said to her, "Whenever a husband isn't attracted to his wife, if he doesn't make her feel like a woman, she finds a man who does. It's a law of nature, true throughout the universe. She develops some petty attraction to a man who makes her feel good about herself. Is there a man like that in your life?" Her husband was sitting right next to her. She became flustered. "No. Of course not. I don't know what you're talking about," she said. I came back. "Look, I'm here with this big crew. We're all here to try to make things better. But if we're not going to be honest with each other, there's no point. Why am I even here? So I'll ask you again, and I don't mean to bully you. But this is important. It's important that your husband understand who you are. Since your husband neglects you and puts you down, is there a man out there whom you turn to who makes you feel good?" She piped up. "Okay, there is someone, but it's innocent. He's a stock boy at the local grocery whose name is Alejandro. He notices my nails whenever I have a manicure. He compliments me on my hair. He is always saying nice things. We're friends, nothing more. But he makes me feel good about myself. And I go to that store to buy the things I need in part because he's there." Amazing. A beautiful woman from a respectable middle-class background. Going to the stock boy because he is the one who gives her a compliment.

Now, how did I know about Alejandro? Am I a prophet? Why yes, I am the *Love* Prophet. But in this case no prophecy was required. You see, women are more emotionally developed than men. Whereas for men, basketball and a Bud Lite might be life's necessities, for women it is affection, attention, and a compliment that provide life's true thrills. The sinful side of this otherwise dignified wife made her erotically desirable before our very eyes. She blossomed as a woman. Which is not to say that she would have ever done anything about it . . . or would she?

Would she? You never know. And that's the whole point. Even the most respectable and pious woman has a sinful side. Which is why her husband better immunize her against falling prey to the guiles of other men by showering infinite affection on her. Happy wife, happy life.

And what about him? Should you get your husband to talk about his petty attractions? Come on. That's gross. Absolutely not. Yes, all men have them. And they're all equally pathetic, a manifestation of weakness and an inability to focus. Because sexual variety in a woman is erotic, while sexual variety in a man is pornographic.

Other sinful ideas: Go to a hotel together. Make love by the window with the blinds open. Try not to get thrown out. (Chances are, no one will be looking anyway. But it sure is erotic).

Take out an Internet alias. Write to your wife on her e-mail account or Facebook. Pretend to be a stranger. Become suggestive. See how she reacts. Her sinfulness will be erotic. Before it goes too far, tell her it's you. In any event, she'll say she knew all along.

Set up a webcam in your bedroom. Tell your wife you've done it. But tell her she'll never know when you're looking. After a while she'll forget it's there. Your wife will become your own private webcam girl. And when you get bored in the office, you can download her rather than downloading pictures of Playmates. Just make sure you don't catch her with the pool guy. Every once in a while remind her that the secret webcam is somewhere in the room. No doubt, she'll find it and cover it with a towel. But that will just spur you to invent an even more daring erotic game. Go on. You're married. Because it's forbidden, it's permitted.

THE FIFTH
SECRET:
OPPOSITES
ATTRACT

You know "that look" women get when they
want sex? Me neither.
—STEVE MARTIN

or eroticism to exist, the sexual polarity between masculine and feminine, our fifth secret, has to be established. Men and women are attracted to each other because they constitute opposing sexual poles. And opposites attract. Opposites complement each other, require one another, and gravitate toward each other. What happens, however, when men and women become too much alike is that the erotic charge is weakened until it is eventually lost. And that is especially troubling in our culture, which is increasingly becoming unisex. Our society overexposes the sexes to one another until sexual difference becomes blighted and neutralized.

In times gone by, men and women were raised apart from each other. From single-sex schools to single-sex swimming pools, men and women had more limited exposure to one another, which increased mystery and also increased sexual polarity. Men and women dressed differently, thought differently, and acted differently (read a Jane Austen novel and you'll see what I'm talking about). Today, however, they do almost everything alike. Sexual separation of old is today dismissed as Victorian, sexist, and primitive. And some of it may have been. But we've gone way too far in the opposite direction. Men wear jeans. Women wear jeans. Men walk around with their boxers showing, women walk around with their thongs showing. Men are ruthlessly ambitious. Women are ruthlessly ambitious. Men lace their language with vulgarity. Women lace their language with vulgarity. Men are commitment-phobic. Women are commitment-phobic.

Not long ago, getting drunk and making an ass of yourself was mostly the preserve of guys. Now we have the *Girls Gone Wild* videos, not to mention Britney Spears and Paris Hilton. Behaving like an idiot is something that both sexes can now share. Clearly, this isn't what we mean by progress.

The vulgar behavior of both men and women is highly nonerotic. Women being defeminized and men becoming degentlemantized subverts erotic attraction. The more alike the sexes become, the less they need each other. Difference is erotic. Sameness is boring.

The erotic mind works through differentiation. Sexual polarity is key. When, say, a husband and wife become too alike, when they do everything together and never have any space, they begin to tire of one another. This is not only due to the loss of novelty, but more importantly to the loss of sexual polarity. This is a strong argument for the need for zones of privacy in marriage. Yes, when we marry we become one flesh. But it's important that we remain one flesh clothed in two bodies. We dare never morph into one person.

Just look at how male and female movie stars who personify sexual polarity retain a hold on the public imagination for decades of their career and usually even after their death. The names are legend. On the male side, Cary Grant, Marlon Brando, and Humphrey Bogart. More recently strong male leads like Al Pacino, Harrison Ford, and Denzel Washington fit the bill. All are distinguished as men known in their roles (for the most part) for chivalry; strong, determined purpose; heroic action; and male ruggedness. The same is true for the female legends of the silver screen. From Lauren Bacall to Rita Hayworth to Sophia Loren to Marilyn Monroe, all are distinguished for sultriness, feminine charm, intelligent flirtatiousness, and womanly form. Gentlemen attract ladies and ladies attract gentlemen.

Erotic attraction grows through the principle of sexual differentiation. There must be tangible differences between the sexes, both covert and overt, in order for erotic polarity to function. This is why the Bible insists on certain incontrovertible differences that must forever remain between men and women. It says that men cannot wear a woman's clothing (Deuteronomy 22:5). Men are not to uproot the hair on their faces (Leviticus 19:27). (Yes, that is the source of my incredibly sexy, scraggly beard.) Even in external appearance, men and women are supposed to look different. In the Jewish religion, men and women sit separately in the synagogue, with a literal divider down the middle, all designed to heighten while not overdoing, the sexual divide.

I am a great believer in single-sex education and would not consider sending my children to a coed school. What happens when kids are overexposed to one another from the earliest age is that they become desensitized to the attraction of the opposite sex. That's why we see coed schools so focused, in their yearbooks and other arenas, on superlatives like, "Most popular," "Most likely to succeed." When I was graduating junior high school, I was amazed that our yearbook had this elitist drivel in it (okay, I was also upset that I was omitted from all the lists). But after some thought it all made sense. Overexposure to the opposite sex made us all ordinary to each other. Because we had become so desensitized to the magic of the opposite sex, the only thing left was to be impressed with those who really stood out. Only superlatives mattered. The most athletic, the best looking. You see the same thing in virtually every high school movie made, where the "ordinary" boys and girls, which constitute 90 percent of the grade, are treated as uninteresting nerds who get wedgies while the quarterback and the head of the cheerleading squad are movie stars. It is incredible how at even an early age, when teenagers are so hormonally charged, they are erotically desensitized to the vast majority of other teenagers, feeling attracted only to about 10 percent of the opposite sex. Single-sex schools are attacked for not allowing boys and girls to learn how to get along with the opposite sex. But more often than not, the opposite is true. A single-sex education leads to boys who are generally interested in crossing the divide and getting to know a girl, while coeducation leads to boys who treat girls like boys, and girls who similarly become inured to the attraction of anything but the most stand-out boys.

This also explains something far more insidious in our culture: the fact that people date and date without falling in love and without getting married. Men and women go out but fail to develop an erotic spark. In my religious community, this rarely happens. On the contrary, most men and women get engaged after dating, perhaps, their fourth or fifth person, maximum, and after dating just a few weeks. I know what you're thinking. Yeah, you religious kooks will marry almost anybody. But give us a bit more credit for our discernment. The real reason they get engaged so much more quickly is that the two sexes have been largely separated since birth. So when they finally go out, they don't need to be impressed with superlatives. They are attracted to good enough—someone who satisfies their needs—as opposed to mounting a fifteen-year search for "the best." When our men and women go out, the date itself is erotic. The differences between men and women are so defined in our community that bringing the two together, even in a nonsexual environment, creates an immediate sexual spark. In short, they go out and guess what? They're actually attracted to each other.

But the secular culture seems intent on blighting difference. Women today understandably aspire to match their male counterparts in all arenas. And so they should. Women are men's equals in most departments, and their superiors in many as well. But one can succeed in a masculine world without embracing negative masculine traits that have undermined men for generations. Women see how blind ambition and aggression can pay off in the workplace, and so they attempt to match it. Like men, they often cultivate blind ambition and are prepared to be ruthless. And women are becoming as good at being domineering and authoritarian as men are. But, as we established earlier, this lust for mastery promotes an acquisitive, masculine mentality and is therefore the antithesis of eroticism, since eroticism is fostered not by the desire to master but by the desire to know.

The carryover of this desire to become more masculine has been expressed in women's growing desire to even *look* more masculine. Every fashion magazine fills their pages with coat hanger models and rail-thin actresses. They may tout the resurgence of curves in their headlines, but the pages in between reveal the truth. Hips are frowned upon and breasts are nonexistent.

It doesn't make sense. On the one hand, the modern world is finally embracing the triumph of feminine over masculine values. The communicative, nurturing, forgiving leader like Nelson Mandela (embracing more feminine qualities) has finally won out over the bloodthirsty conquerors like Ghengis Khan and Saddam Hussein as archetypes of greatness. Gay men on *Queer Eye for the Straight Guy* are, amazingly, becoming the instructors of straight men, teaching them how to dress, be more domesticated, and please a woman. Biology reveals its own clue: We are all female until forty days after gestation. That's a pretty great big hint from G-d about the fundamental primacy of the feminine. Yes, there is a need for male aggression. But ultimately, all masculinity must be tempered by the feminine.

This is the reason why, unlike other religions, Judaism insists on marriage. By marriage, I do not only mean the institution, but rather the softening of the masculine by exposure to the feminine, the amelioration of the aggressive through synthesis with the passive. Judaism insists on curbing the desire for conquest with the desire for peace. We glorify the Sabbath, a passive day of peace and rest, as our holiest day as a way of curtailing out-of-control ambition and soulless capitalism. We have strict prohibitions on eating blood, and are prohibited from eating animals or birds of prey.

The ancient world glorified warriors like Odysseus, Agamemnon, Hannibal, and Caesar. But the Jews glorify Abraham, who is praised in the Bible for being a caterer; Jacob, who pardons the angel with whom he struggles; and Joseph, who forgives his brothers their attempt at fratricide.

Even King David, our greatest warrior, is celebrated not for his military triumphs but for playing harp and lyre and authoring the moving Psalms. Even so, David could not build the Temple because he was a man of war.

And yet, in today's Western world, femininity is still seen primarily as a weakness. Politicians all want to demonstrate that they have the killer instinct to be president. Female executives want to demonstrate that rather than managing with a softer gentler approach, they are fully capable of being iron like their male counterparts.

Anatomically men are lines and women are circles. And this does not merely reflect their genitals, but their general approach to life. Men are goal-oriented, women primarily means-oriented. Men, in bed, rush to the finish line; women love extended foreplay. But the perfect male is someone who becomes a bit of a curve, giving up his rigidity and the line's natural fear of being trapped in a circle, aka, commitment-phobia.

I spoke with a female friend of mine who lamented the roundness of her face and fullness of her cheeks. She complained that she would never be photogenic because she had no cheekbones. I was taken aback. Her complete acceptance of the linear perspective, that full and round was bad and lean and angular was desirable, fully prevented her from seeing beauty in a softer, more classical light. She was a circle trying to be a line. And while she could be a happy and natural circle, she would do anything to force herself into the skin of a line.

Women have to re-embrace the circle. They must stop seeking to mirror the line, all lanky and gaunt, prone to achieving and hurting. We need to restore to its proper value the nurturing and regenerative properties of a circle. In fact, we need to incorporate circle-like qualities within our lines. Doing so will allow for the lines to become a hook, so like Velcro they will allow for connections that last and endure, not simply sliding away as two lines making contact are known to do.

Men also lose out when women begin to think like men. Western sexuality leads to compartmentalization, a distillation of sex into an act, where you are judged on your size and performance and not for who you are. In an arena where men can be allowed to let their innermost being manifest, they are still being treated like they're in a boardroom, where their offerings are carefully measured and evaluated.

Men also have to embrace the circle because, being so

linear, they don't get the most of love and sex. Relationships hit an endpoint. They begin to feel restless. There is a feminine, circular dimension in men that must be embraced and brought to the fore. They have to learn how to find renewal within the same relationship. Think of it as men transforming from being a line into being more of a curve. They can still be goal-oriented, the man-with-the-plan. But they need not be so rigid, so harsh, so set on rushing to the finish line. They can enjoy the journey. Love can't be masculine. It involves bringing out the nurturer within us, the part of us that needs compassion and emotional nurturing, allowing men to be vulnerable and emotionally available.

But this does not mean that men should not be men. It simply means that a man can exhibit raw masculinity while still allowing his wife to take the lead in bed. After all, when the line and the circle are finally joined in the closest possible embrace in sex, notice that the line is enveloped by a circle. The circle comes out on top.

But amid men learning from their wives how to enjoy things like domestication, children, and foreplay, they should still not morph into their wives or the wives into their husbands, which is an even bigger problem today as women become more masculine. Husbands and wives need to recapture some of that same erotic longing by ensuring they never grow into being the same as each other and always maintain erotic differentiation.

One of the best ways to ensure this erotic differentiation is for men to once again become gentlemen and for women to become ladies. No, I'm not advocating that men wear britches and women put on rib-crushing corsets. But one of the reasons we love watching period dramas, or Jane Austen films, is because of the erotic charge that always seems to exist between the men and women. Yes, I know that Victorians have become metaphors for sexual repression and hypocrisy and I'm not asking that any of us go back to a time when women were treated as porcelain dolls. I've got six daughters, for goodness' sake, and I want them to have every opportunity that a man has to use their brains and G-d-given talent to make a positive impact on the world. But the reason these period dramas are so naturally romantic is that the differentiation between the sexes is so strongly pronounced. The men are gentlemen; the women are ladies. There is a certain refinement of character that each possesses. And if husbands and wives would act more accordingly, the erotic spark between them would naturally grow.

Would it really hurt if husbands always took showers at night before getting in bed with their wives? Would it be a big deal if they didn't burp or pick their noses in front of their wives? When men dress like gentlemen, it also increases the erotic attraction that women have for them. But in our country, that rarely happens. I remember a *Newsweek* cover from a number of years ago entitled, "Nation of Slobs." It showed a picture of fans at a football game dressed, well, like slobs. Look, I like dressing casually as well. But surely if you're taking your wife out for dinner you can put on a jacket or at least a finely pressed shirt. And no, a belch does not count as offering her something of your innermost self.

But the same is true in reverse. Women who act like ladies

increase erotic pull. Going to the bathroom in front of your husband is gross. Taking care of any of your feminine hygiene requirements is the same. Using vulgar language is *not* becoming to a lady. Not everything in marriage is meant to be shared. Do it in private. Britney Spears can flash her privates all she wants. But people will look because of its shock effect rather than any real erotic interest. In behaving like anything but a lady, she took a naturally erotic part of her body and made it first plain, and then unseemly. People felt sorry for her. And she is destroying her career in the process. Who wants to see this garbage? But for us lesser mortals, surely if your husband is taking you to the theater you can put on an attractive dress rather than wear the torn jeans you did around the house.

I once counseled Jill, who laced nearly all of her language with profanities. I asked her if she felt that her husband would be attracted to a truck driver. She admitted that she never saw it that way and vowed to stop. By gentlemanly we also mean romantic. The romantic husband creates an erotic spark with his wife. When he opens doors for her, takes her hand as they walk down the street, buys her romantic objects like flowers and perfume, he creates desire. Embracing the role of the erotic suitor increases her attraction to him. Not only because women love romance, but because his gentlemanly behavior promotes erotic differentiation. He is behaving like a man and in so doing he creates an electric spark with the woman in his life.

The same is true of dressing differently. It's amazing, husbands and wives will dress up for the whole world, but not for each other. Around one another they dress the same. Both are wearing T-shirts and sweatpants. Now, you don't have to wear ball gowns walking around the home. But something slightly more ladylike than a stained T-shirt isn't asking all that much. And yes, you have a right to be casual in your home around your spouse. But sometimes, smart casual is a more erotic choice.

Leslie and Charles came to me for marital counseling after their marriage was upended by the birth of a baby boy. Charles felt he had lost his wife to his own son. Leslie, an attractive woman in her thirties, walked around in sweats the entire day. She ceased putting on any makeup. Charles was frustrated. "Is that it? We become parents and good-bye to our relationship?" Leslie responded, "I'm just so tired. Why should I get dressed up? We're not going out anywhere. I still have to be home with the baby."

I said to her, "You mean, Leslie, that all these years when you got dressed up to go out you were only doing so for strangers?" I then told Charles that rather than getting frustrated he should do two things. "First, take your wife out to shop for clothes. Go with her. Tell her what makes her look sexy. Second, do more work around the house so that your wife is less tired and more amorous."

Other ideas to increase sexual polarity: Wives should wear lacy undergarments. Get rid of the utilitarian bra. Lace is profoundly feminine, which is why you won't find it in Fruit of the Loom underwear. One of the biggest giveaways that a wife is having an affair is when she changes from cotton undergarments to silk. And make sure your husband sees the lacy bra, only don't do it intentionally. It should always be something he notices quite casually as you go about your daily business. This makes it more sinful.

Husbands: Take good care of your wives. If she's not feeling well, bring her breakfast in bed. Do the dishes for her. Make her tea. The more you show caring for your wife, the more you establish yourself as the radiant knight who offers her protection. I have heard countless wives tell me, "I take care of everyone else, but there is no one to take care of me." No matter how independent a woman is, she will always feel attraction for the man who takes good care of her.

Another idea: In Jewish law, this one is important. During marital sex a husband should always ensure that his wife climaxes first. Not only is this chivalrous and gentlemanly, but it establishes sexual polarity by allowing a husband to focus on his wife's erotic response. Women, as I have consistently maintained, are much more sexual than men. A woman in the throes of sexual ecstasy arouses her husband like nothing else. She experiences total abandonment and the force of her sexual crescendo renders her all but lifeless. Any husband who sees his wife in this state can never forget that she is not a friend, nor some drinking buddy, but a woman of vast sexual power.

The vast power of sexual force I just described leads us to our sixth secret of eroticism. In the next chapter, we'll explore the necessity of reckless abandon to spark Eros in our marriages.

THE SIXTH
SECRET:
RECKLESS
ABANDON

I don't think when I make love.
　　　　　　　　　　　—Brigette Bardot

ℛeckless erotic abandon is reached when you experience something so thrilling, so electrifying, so overwhelming, that you cannot help but submit to it completely. There can be no resistance. This is why eroticism is so often associated with pain and sin. Why is sadomasochism associated with Eros? Because pain, for some, is one of the only ways to gauge whether they are experiencing something so erotically electrifying that they submit to it completely. Man, having this boiling wax dripped onto my skin sure hurts, but damn me if it isn't exciting (I'm just using a far-out example here). It hurts to have this stuff done to you, and in a normal, everyday context, not only would you not pay for it, you would call the police on anyone who subjected you to it. But in an erotic context it becomes something so powerful that pain turns into pleasure. When this stuff was done to prisoners in Abu Ghraib prison in Baghdad, it rightly elicited international condemnation for torture. But when men and women do this to each other in an erotic context, it's called pleasure. Even as it kills your body to have someone lash you with a bullwhip, you ask for more. You have abandoned yourself utterly to the erotic pleasure.

But then there is another part of us, a passionate part that is raw, instinctive, animal, visceral, and not attuned to societal norms. It is the part of us that, in an erotic situation, submits entirely to instinct and loses all control. It's the part of us that really couldn't give a damn what people think and throws caution to the wind. And it's incredibly erotic to witness this side of a person become revealed. A man who can arouse a woman to this level of abandonment witnesses something incredible. Her real sexual self is now manifest without any societal constraints. This is the real her, the part of her that was always yearning to break free of the chains of restraint. She is now more alive than she has even been, and he is the cause. Smokin'!

This visceral, organic side of our personality is the most private part of ourselves, the real us, the part that is uncalculating, intuitive, uninhibited, authentic, and totally human. To be sure, it's not always pretty and it does need to be cultured and civilized. It does not conform to social expectations and indeed is governed not by the mind but by impulse. And yet, it's equally unhealthy to become so detached from it that we can no longer draw on its herculean power. Few people these days ever discover this part of themselves. They lead controlled lives that so utterly conform to the standards the world expects of them that their innermost self becomes compromised.

And that's where eroticism comes in. Eroticism is the ability to experience such utter abandonment that your truest self is manifest. Eroticism involves experiencing life at its rawest and most intense. And it has the power to make you feel more than you ever thought possible. When you see that side of your spouse through the intimacy of the carnal, you are finally witnessing their truest self. Eroticism has helped to scrape away all the pretentious layers and you get to witness their irreducible essence.

I have counseled many wives who had chosen to have an affair, and a majority said they made that tragic decision because they would have died had they not. And what they meant by that was not only that being ignored by their husbands made them feel like they didn't matter, but also that they had lost touch with that raw, animal self. They had forgotten how it felt to feel completely alive. They were running on autopilot. They went from being single women who were alive and liked to smile to being housewives entirely encumbered by responsibility. And great marital sex, which could have brought them to life amid those responsibilities, was usually perfunctory or nonexistent, with the result being that they slowly lost touch of their inner selves.

Maggie was an example. Married to an accountant who was setting up his own business, she embraced the traditional role of a housewife and quickly had three kids. Her husband traveled constantly and when he came home at night he was usually too tired to speak to her about anything other than practical matters. Sex was about once a week and was uninspiring. When she met a man at a Starbucks who struck up a conversation with her (which is not surprising, given that lonely married women can be spotted from a million miles away), she felt exhilarated but understandably wary. After a few phone calls, she swore to herself that she would end the fledgling affair. But she couldn't. He was a magnet, drawing her close. The affair became full-blown and after six months, racked with guilt, she confessed to her husband, who completely lost it and called all her friends to tell them what a "slut and a whore" she was. It was left for me to pick up the pieces of this broken marriage when they finally came to me for counseling. I failed, and they divorced a few months later. But what I remember most from my conversations with them was Maggie telling me how odd it felt to go home to her husband every night and know that he did not know her. That a stranger she was having passionate sex with knew her so much better than her own husband, with whom she lived and had children. The stranger brought out the real her, the alive woman she had once been. To her husband she was the cook and the cleaner.

In marriage it is our spouse who is supposed to invite us into this erotic modality and witness us in this state. It is the intimate sexual experience of two people who love each other deeply that has the power to scrape away the thick layer of social convention under which we all hide. And it is the person who sees us in that state and who shares that state with us who knows us in a way that nobody else can. It is also that person to whom we become connected and indebted for simply setting us free. You may be concealed from the whole world, but there is one person whom you invite into your most private arena, your most intimate space, and who sees you with no embellishment. But if your marriage is not passionate or erotic, then your public self remains on display even in your relationship. Even in the privacy of your own bedroom, you remain metaphorically clothed. All your pretentions are still there and you mask your innermost self even from your own spouse. You remain a prisoner even in the comfort of your own home. This explains why so many husbands and wives simply fail to achieve the intimacy that would bring happiness. Without erotic passion, there can be no intimate bonding.

I saw this play out in the marriage of Kevin and Marcia. Their marriage had great love and trust, but Marcia still felt unhappy. She felt there was something missing, but it was not something obvious. They weren't bonding as deeply as she had hoped. In counseling it quickly emerged that their sex life was routine and uninspiring. It also emerged that in a previous relationship Marcia had an extremely passionate sex life with a man with whom she had little else in common. She left that relationship because she felt that she and her boyfriend were incompatible. She was much closer to her husband than to her boyfriend, but still she felt she had left something behind in the previous relationship that this one lacked.

The advice I gave her was simple: "What you left behind was not something merely sexual. It was your authentic self. What you're feeling is that your ex-boyfriend saw a part of you that no one had seen, including your husband. He awakened a raw animal carnality that has since become submerged.

Now, you feel odd that a stranger knows you better than your husband. And that's why you and your husband need to bring erotic passion into this relationship. You thought you'd be intimate just by living as best friends. Now you realize that even friends live according to conventions, but lovers live by instinct."

We're not meant to be strangers in marriage. We're supposed to know each other deeply. It's essential that a man come to know his wife intimately, and vice versa. A husband must discover which sexual positions his wife finds thrilling and fantasizes about. Too many husbands allow their sexual rhythm to fall into a routine. Simply put, they get lazy. As I have consistently maintained, women are much more sexual than men. And while men are usually satisfied to have marital sex in the missionary position, their wives more often than not are more inwardly adventurous. But they don't share the fantasy for all kinds of reasons. They're embarrassed, they don't think it would make a difference, or they, too, have become complacent. To remedy this, a husband should arouse his wife—through kissing, foreplay, an erotic massage—to the point that she is an erotic mood and is ready to share her fantasies. Ask her what positions she loves. And once you're in the position, ask her how she is feeling. The more she describes her pleasure, the more she will feel it. Words have the power to excite emotions. And the more she feels it, the more her inner, fiery nature will come out. It's an amazing thing for a husband to watch. I know one wife whose fantasy was for her husband to hold her breasts while he made love to her from behind. She held that fantasy in for fifteen years and used it to pleasure herself. She never once shared with her husband because she said every night he would just climb on top of her in the missionary position and that was their sex life. That was fifteen lost years when he could have witnessed his wife's animal instincts.

A wife should, during sex, ask her husband what he wants her to do to him. I say during sex because it is specifically during arousal that the inner animal starts to come alive. The social filter through which we do things begins to recede. Often, he won't respond immediately because he is immersed in his own world of fantasy and finds the conversation to be distracting. Tough. He shouldn't be in his own private fantasy world. The idea is for you to join him there. In that fantasy world lies his authentic nature, which remains concealed. Your job is to open him up. If he is not forthcoming with sharing his fantasies of what he would like you to do, start making suggestions. Ask him, "Would you like me to do X?" "Would you like to see me doing Y?" Soon enough, he'll begin to respond and his passion will overtake him.

Husbands, from time to time, buy your wife kinky lingerie and just spring it on her; or wives, bring your husband some new sex toy and ask him to try it on you. In the same spirit, have a drink before sex. Loosen up. Purge yourself of inhibition. And finally, use sex to mend a heated argument.

Okay, I know that bunching these last four suggestions together seems pretty weird. So let me explain. The Talmud says that there are four ways to know the true, inner person. Four ways to scrape away the outer, superficial layers and expose the human soul: look at what the person spends their money on; what a person says when they drink; what a person says when they are angry; and how a person spends their leisure time.

What you spend your money on captures what you consider of value. All too often we spend our money on luxury items, thereby demonstrating that we are shallow materialists. But when a husband risks the embarrassment of going into a lingerie store and buying his wife a sexy bra or underwear, he is showing that what is really on his mind, what his inner nature craves, is erotic sex with his wife. In other words, *she* is on his mind. And only she can bring out his inner, animal nature. Conversely, when a wife goes out and buys a sex device and asks her husband to use it on her, she is showing him her inner, instinctual self. She desires great sexual pleasure and wants her husband to be the one who brings her sexual joy and satisfaction. She is not someone who merely washes dishes and does the laundry. She is a seductress.

Likewise, what a person says when they are drunk or angry is their truest self because in both instances they remove the social filter that usually guards their words. Now, anger is obviously not conducive to sex. And truth be told, you should never get angry because anger is always a loss of control. But to the extent that in marriage we sometimes have heated arguments and our inner rage is about to be let loose, think to yourself, *This is the perfect opportunity for erotic sex. Rather than allowing myself to blow a gasket at my spouse and have some stupid argument, I'm going to use that swelling passion to create glorious intimacy.* And then channel that swelling anger into sexual passion. It works. Your spouse will be confused that you looked so angry a moment ago and now you want to make passionate love to them. So explain it. "I was getting angry. But whenever I feel intense emotion, it brings to life this inner animal in me that just wants to take you because I need you so badly."

Drunkenness is a bad thing, so never overdo it. But a glass of wine before sex will help you let go of inhibition and allow your unrestrained desire to be manifest.

Marriage sometimes involves breaking the rules. You have to push the boundaries. Watching a porn tape together is not what I mean. That's a cop-out, needing to rely on strangers and compromising the intimacy of your marriage in order to find some passion. But your wife may be particularly sensitive on her earlobes. She may stop you whenever you blow on them. Her stomach may be her most sensitive part. Well, don't be afraid of providing sensory overload. She'll try to stop you. She may even get ticklish and laugh. But don't stop. Bring her to a point of arousal where she can no longer make you stop.

Another suggestion for tapping into sexual abandon— during sex, tell your wife you want her to scream. You want to hear her shout her yearning out loud. She'll initially feel self-conscious. And in any event, aren't you the one who is supposed to make her scream, without even wanting to? No matter. Articulating sound actually increases desire and abandonment. Look at the most passionate fans at a football game. The more they cheer, the more they get into the game.

This is not a sex book, but an eroticism book. As such, I have touched on overt sexuality only when the situation calls for it. This is one of those instances. Sexual abandonment is most experienced in rough sex. Many men have the impression that their wives only want soft erotic massages and deep, intimate kissing. Well, that's part of what they want. But if that were all, it could not explain the vast number of women who confess to rape fantasies. Now, no woman wants to be raped, an act of criminal violence that is an utter abomination. But your wife does want to be taken. And being taken means that she wants you, at times, to overpower her, to make love to her with intensity and ferocity. Indeed, at times, love does *not* feel like it should. You do have to make it hurt so good. Wives who have had lovers often report that what made the sex exciting was that it was so much rougher than marital sex. It's not radically different to our tastes in food. Sometimes we love sweet food, and sometimes sharp, savory food. The same is true of sex. So go ahead and take her. Fling her around the bed and make passionate love to her. It's okay. You're married. It's forbidden, therefore it's allowed. When she asks what came over you as she slowly watches Dr. David Banner turn into the Incredible Hulk, tell her it's your irresistible lust for her. She makes you crazy with desire, like every wife should.

THE SEVENTH
SECRET:
UNQUENCHABLE
YEARNING

I adjure you, O daughters of Jerusalem,
If you find my beloved,
That you tell him that I am sick from love....
Many waters cannot quench love,
neither can the floods drown it.
—SONG OF SOLOMON, 5:8; 8:7

$\mathscr{H}$ere's the rule: bad sex involves instant gratification. Good sex involves delayed gratification. And erotic sex involves our seventh secret, unquenchable yearning.

To explain: Bad sex is where you pursue instant gratification. Premature ejaculation, which many men struggle to control, is an example. So is quickie sex where both husband and wife are left utterly unsatisfied. Sadly, all too many husbands pursue just that. They're lazy lovers. They're satisfied with a boring orgasm, even though their wives get to feel satisfied once every blue moon, which explains the famous statistic that the rate of husband-to-wife orgasm in sex is about eight to one.

Our culture is designed for instant gratification so that no inner urge is left unscratched. Hungry? Pick up the phone and a pizza is delivered lickety-split. Forget that we had dinner just an hour ago and there is nothing wrong with feeling a bit hungry. It's healthy. But not for us. When our belly calls we run to silence it. Quash the pang. Scratch the itch. Calm the tension, however unhealthy it may be.

But nowhere is this truer than with sex. We treat sex as a biological urge that needs to be satiated. We have to get rid of the urge by indulging the craving. Americans seem to have lost all sexual control. In a strange sort of way, they have sex in order *not to want to have sex*. It's not radically different than dinner. We eat in order to stop eating, to stop feeling hungry, to lose our appetite. Likewise, we use sex to anesthetize our craving. This is sex as an all-natural sleeping pill. It's like having a stiff drink. It relaxes us. There is an apocryphal story that prior to his famous presidential debate with Richard Nixon, JFK had a woman brought to him and had sex. Apparently, so the legend goes, he did so whenever he had important speeches to give. He told his aides that sex relaxed him. But that's why JFK, according to the women who claimed to be his lovers and wrote memoirs of their relationship, was a terrible lover. A few minutes of sex and he was done. Sex and women were used to relieve pressure. Nixon did the same thing with a drink, prompting his secretary of state, Henry Kissinger, to refer to his boss, the president, as "our drunken friend." Everyone has their own way to blow off steam.

A player friend of mine related to me that although he was very happy with his new girlfriend, he had still cheated on her numerous times. When I asked him why, he said, matter-of-factly, "To satisfy my urges." Here was a man who was both controlled by his urges and did his best to quiet them. Then there was Harold who told me over dinner with his wife that, "Sex helps me fall asleep. If you don't believe me, just ask my wife." His wife nodded in amused agreement and added, "He sleeps like the dead after sex." I thought to myself of how badly their sex life could use a resurrection.

For those, especially women, wishing to discern, therefore, whether the sex they are having is good or bad, intimate or distant, selfish or loving, the questions are these:

Do you look into each other's eyes or close them?

Do you kiss for a long time during sex, or is kissing mostly absent?

Is sexual climax with eyes open or closed?

Does sex take the national average, three to seven minutes, or is it prolonged?

Do you feel closer when sex is over, or do you simply feel tired and ready for sleep?

Good sex involves delayed gratification. You don't just jump straight to intercourse. You engage in passionate kissing, long foreplay, and you build up desire. Only then do you consummate that desire by actually making love.

But the highest category, eroticism, or what we call great sex, goes beyond delayed gratification and involves unquenchable yearning, longing, and lusting after something who's always just in front of you but whom you can never quite reach. It's the husband and wife who have sex for a few nights straight without climax, always building greater desire, always heightening erotic longing. It's the husband and wife who take turns giving each other long and deeply arousing erotic massages, resisting the urge to have sex, holding out the promise of more.

Sociologists point out that the definition of maturity is delayed gratification. A child needs everything right now. It's the reason they love candy rather than a healthy salad. The instant sweet taste is enticing to their palate. Only with time will they acquire higher tastes by delaying gratification. Whereas today they love the taste of Coke, years down the line they will come to appreciate a fine wine. Sex is the same. There are boys and men. The boys want an orgasm, right now, and use their wives to obtain it. Their sex life is deplorable and even worse for their wives. The men are prepared to delay gratification and engage in extended foreplay.

But then, there are the philosophers, and they have not only delayed gratification but sexual wisdom. The sexual philosopher wants to harness sexuality to understand his or her deeper nature. They are prepared not only to delay lovemaking for an hour, but to delay orgasm for a week or more. They have sex without climax so as to arouse the strongest sexual urge until they are transformed from having sex to living erotically.

When I was a boy I used to love watching *The Little Rascals*. The way they would move around was by using an old buggy that was drawn by a half-burned-out mule. In front of the mule's face hung a carrot held up by a fishing pole. The carrot was always dangling in front of the mule, and the mule would chase it, forever elusively, forever frustrated. Chasing that prize is what kept the half-dead beast going.

Eroticism is based on the same principle. It is something that is dangled before the inner beast, our animal energy, but try as you might you can never quite grasp it. And the moment you do, it ceases to be erotic. It is much like a secret that you long to hear. As soon as its contents are revealed, it has ceased to be a secret and in the process it has ceased to be interesting or erotic.

Unquenchable desire is the reason why adultery is so erotic. You can never fully have your sexual partner, seeing that they are married to someone else. At any moment they can be taken away from you. When you do have them, you have done so only partially. Their foremost allegiance is still to someone else.

The way we bring unquenchable desire into a marriage is first and foremost to have a biblically-mandated period of sexual separation in the marriage, as discussed in previous chapters. Knowing you can't have each other lets you yearn and lust for one another. A husband's desire for his wife slow burns to a fever pitch.

But there is more. Husbands and wives should learn to talk openly about what erotic desires they have. Not just fantasy—things they know they'll never do and which they leave in the realm of fantasy—but rather things they wish they could do, but are too shy to execute. Every husband and wife has some wild sex idea they want to do, but, out of modesty or shame or fear, keep it to themselves. But there is no room for that kind of inhibition in marriage. Sexy conversations lead to burning passion and desire.

A good time to practice this is when either husband or wife is traveling. Have phone sex with your wife. Let your desire for each other cajole some great and previously undisclosed sexual conversation from one another. Don't masturbate on the phone. That kills the exercise. The idea is to build up, rather than release, your sexual desire so that by the time you are reunited you are ripping each other's clothes off.

Melissa was a wife feeling bored with her husband. Their sex life was routine and uninspiring. She saw him in the same light. She told me he was anal retentive, an in-the-box kind of guy who just didn't turn her on. Their rate of sexual frequency was relatively high, about twice a week, double the national average. But it was always in the missionary position and it lasted for about five minutes. I told her that when it came to sex, there is no such thing as an in-the-box kind of man or woman. Every man and woman has an inner sexual fire. It is just a question of who or what brings it out. Yes, I actually believe this, which is why the idea of sexual compatibility is such a farce. Sexual compatibility, as I have often said, is nothing but an excuse used by lazy lovers who won't do the work necessary to bring out their partners' nascent sexual fire.

I encouraged Melissa to push her husband, to explore what fire lurked under the ice. Walking through their neighborhood one day, she asked what crazy sexual scenarios he had in mind that they had never done. He blushed. She asked again. He indicated he wasn't comfortable with the conversation, especially outdoors. She demanded an answer. He said he had always wanted to take nude pictures of her and keep them password-protected on his laptop. Now she was the prude. She felt self-conscious. He cajoled her. They took the pictures. But that's not even the point. The real point is this bored woman discovered that underneath her husband had real unquenchable erotic desire. He wanted his wife as his own personal porn star. And there's nothing wrong with that. As long as it's your wife.

Another man told me a similar thing about his marriage. Routine, boredom, bad sex, the usual. I told him to push his wife to discover what new sexual position she always wanted to experience. Reluctantly, he had the conversation. It did not take much cajoling for his wife to tell him that she always wanted to ride naked on a horse, with a man riding right behind her on the same saddle. Okay, it sounds crazy, but they actualized the fantasy, renting horses for a day and when they got to a private clearing, everything came off. But again, that's not the point. Because even after having realized this particular fantasy, there would have been another, a newer, more exciting scenario welling up from her loins. Because she was a woman, and her desire was utterly unquenchable. And it's when we discover this aspect of our spouse that we build within them an unbreakable erotic bond.

Ask your wife about the men she dated before she married you. Which ones did she consider husband material? Which ones does she still miss? As she tells you, imagine the unquenchable desire she has for these men as she discusses them. They are lost to her forever. She experiences unquenchable yearning for them. Now, how can you take those qualities and bring them on to you, so that you and your wife can experience a taste of that same yearning? What qualities do they possess that you lack? Perhaps your wife said that one of them was a real romantic. Another was the most attentive lover. Another confessed his deepest fears. Do the same thing. And you wives, don't be afraid to open up about those previous attachments. It may hurt your husband to feel compared, but when he discovers that fragments of your heart still belong to someone else, that gives him the yearning to possess you completely. Being unable to have you fully is what makes him insatiable for you. No matter how much he has you he still doesn't have you.

Kiss for a full hour before you move on to anything sexual. Kissing is that aspect of human intimacy that creates the strongest desire. It is a literal exchange of life-breaths and gives you a glimpse of what it's like to become one soul, one spirit. Notice the difference between kissing and sex. When you have sex, you reach a crescendo and then you lose interest. Your energy has been expunged and you become sleepy. Not so with kissing where there is no climax. The more you kiss, the more you want to kiss. The more you kiss the more intimate it becomes. In simply pressing your lips against your spouse and allowing arousal to build, you begin to experience unquenchable desire to be as close as possible to your spouse. If you allow kissing to be truly prolonged, then sex has a different texture. It is more intimate, more pleasurable, and its effects don't wear off nearly as fast.

Let's move on to our final and most alluring secret of eroticism. This secret exists beyond the body in the expansion of your consciousness. I promise it will blow your mind.

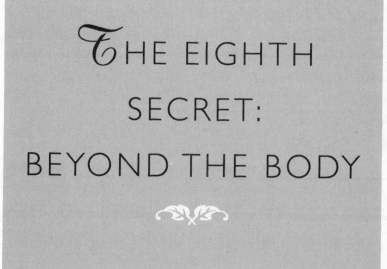

THE EIGHTH SECRET: BEYOND THE BODY

*One word frees us of all the weight and pain
of life; that word is love.*
—SOPHOCLES

*W*omen who have had an incredibly potent erotic experience will often tell you that they saw colors. This is a product of the expansion of consciousness that is the hallmark of true eroticism and sexual climax. And it doesn't matter if you don't literally see colors. The point is that you feel a socket being blown in your mind. Your head is being pushed beyond its limits. You're entering a higher realm than you ever knew existed.

Expansion of consciousness means that your horizons have expanded. What you thought to be the limits of human pleasure have been obliterated. You have seen past the edge. Rigid existence has become malleable. You have entered a realm of pure, sheer presence. You feel more alive than ever before. There is no past; there is no future. You are so present that there is only the here and now. You are no longer calculating your actions, no longer calculating your response. You have reached a point of sheer intuition. Things happen automatically. You have become your inner life-force. You are flesh incarnate.

This is the realm of absolute being rather than doing. At this level of erotic excitement, you cannot think, you cannot ponder, you cannot act, and you cannot do. Intuition has completely taken over. Conscious thought has receded into the dark space of the past. You are in the present and now you can only experience. You are rendered utterly passive as the most potent wave of energy takes over every part of your being. Indeed, you often cannot speak, and are reduced to inarticulate sounds; the more powerful the feelings, the less they can be expressed by words. The conscious act and the limitations of speech just will not do. When we speak of the true sounds of sex, this is what we mean.

This brings us to the following question: which is the true human temple? The body or the soul? In the minds of most people, the body is vastly inferior to the soul, which is why religious people in particular often have a hard time respecting sex. Since sex is of the body, it can't possibly be a godly act. And it would, indeed, seem a logical assumption that in order to please G-d, we must first attend to the needs of the soul. After all, how can the body, the outer trappings of flesh, be important when G-d himself has none? Clearly the bones and sinews and blood and guts were simply an afterthought. It is the soul that merits attention.

So if we want to "talk shop" with G-d, when and if we ever get the chance to do so, we will want to reveal to him that we have spent precious time and energy developing our inner self, even if it is at the sacrifice of our outer self. This is our tendency in everyday life as well. We meet a doctor, we tell him about the article we read about heart valves in the science section of the *Times*. We meet a musician and we discuss the last concert we attended at Lincoln Center. We find the common ground, and we assume that this is what should be discussed. With G-d, our common ground is spirituality.

So, the thinking goes, with sex and love. Sex is the animal part of us. Love, the uniquely human. So sex can't be that important in a relationship. I've heard this argument made a million times, particularly by married couples who have ceased having sex.

And yet there is a flaw in this thinking. For G-d is not simply spiritual. He has found physical expression in the creation of the world and the physical realm. Indeed, this is perhaps the most common of all religious errors, the belief that G-d is to be found more in the heavens than he is on earth, belying the truth spoken by the Bible that "all the earth is filled with His glory." G-d is spirit, and G-d is flesh. G-d is spiritual, and G-d also creates the physical. Possessing no limitations, he is *in*-finite, which is another way of saying that declaring him to be pure spirit would be just as limiting as saying he has a body. This ability, to be both ethereal and tangible, to fill the heavens and also the earth, is his most miraculous quality. The same G-d who creates the soul also creates the body, the latter being no less holy than the former.

To denigrate sex as being "ungodly" is patently absurd and confines G-d to the realm of the spirit when he is equally the G-d of flesh. Therefore, husbands and wives who allow their sex lives to dry up have effectively allowed their love to shrivel. They have no means by which to take the lofty ideal of love and express it in the most tangible, earthly form. For just as G-d's infinite is expressed in his ability to reach all the way down from the heavens and make his creative power manifest here on earth, likewise a man and woman's love for each other expresses itself in its ability to leave the lofty realm of the heart and be manifest in the fleshiness of the carnal embrace. In sum, sex is love incarnate.

If love were something limited only to the spiritual, then it could be expressed only through transcendent pursuits, things like thought and speech and meditation. It could never be expressed through touch. But that would just demonstrate its powerlessness. Because the more potent a thing is, the more able it is to reach from the highest heights to the lowest depths. The better technology a company possesses, the more it is able to miniaturize its technology into a neat little package. What impressed everyone about the Apple iPhone was the ability to stuff so much neat technology into one tiny little device. A few years ago, before the technology was so advanced, cell phones had a fraction of the features and required a crane to lift onto one's shoulder to make a call. Likewise, the more computer technology advances, the more transistors they are able to squeeze onto a wafer-like, silicon chip. Conversely, a man as smart as Albert Einstein is able to teach relativity to college professors. But in his genius he is also able to bring it down to the level of schoolchildren. The range of his genius enables him to reach all the way down. The smarter you are, the more you can condense.

The same is true of sex. The power of human love is expressed in its ability to permeate even our outermost layers. Not just our soul, but even our skin. Lovemaking is so powerful that it can be felt specifically in those external zones, our bodies. If it could be only felt in the mind and heart, it would prove just how weak it is. That's how we know that sex is the most powerful of all human endeavors. Nothing grips us like sex. It grabs the totality of who we are. Unlike almost every other human endeavor, it consumes us completely.

To achieve a state where the spiritual and physical coexist, where the love of the heart is expressed in the touch of the hands, is to experience the raw power of life. It is to feel godly, which is why, as numerous studies have shown, the most common refrain of men and women in the throes of sexual ecstasy, is to scream, "Oh my G-d, oh my G-d." Our natural divinity is manifest.

This is what a sexual union should aspire to be. The physical act of sex is the key to a spiritual awakening that can happen within us, that nothing else has the power to unlock. It should never be "just sex." That is wasting a force that is too precious and too powerful.

Taken further, we see that not only is sex the use of a physical act to unlock the spiritual, but it is the use of a raw and seemingly aggressive act to release something subtle. Sex releases and expresses love. Again—the theory of opposites. Invasion becomes love. Pain becomes pleasure. A thrust brings out tenderness. As John Mellencamp said, truly passionate lovemaking is where "you make it hurt so good."

Like a detonated bomb, the massive physical energy that goes into sexual intercourse transforms into another powerful force—an ethereal force of emotion and feeling. It is consistent with the law of physics: mass and energy are one. Sex is the physical act that is needed to serve as a catalyst for the reaction that will release the congealed spirit that makes up our humanity. The physical allows us to "tap in." The material world opens us and releases the spiritual.

Eroticism's apogee is the experiencing of a vast expansion of consciousness. As the natural by-product of participating in an explosive erotic encounter, you feel more alert than you ever have before. All without making any effort. At this level, you and your spouse fuse into one being, one indivisible energy unit. You become not just one bone and one flesh, but one life-force. The defined boundaries of where you stop and where he begins are erased. The pleasure coursing through the two of you is so strong that it sears and fuses you together, like two pieces of metal that melt into one. At this level a couple is sewn together inseparably. They experience a level of emotional arousal that is so overwhelming that it washes them together to a shared promised land of infinite togetherness.

A woman never forgets a man who brings her to this place. She never forgets he who triggers that level of emotion and expanded consciousness. She connects to the experience forever. Likewise, a man can develop lifelong excitement from the memory of witnessing the wife he loves reach that place. This is marital sex with a nuclear detonation, the conversion of sexual into pure erotic energy.

So often in life we ask ourselves, *Is this as good as it gets?* Work, responsibility, occasional joy, professional pressures, bills, worries about the kids. Do you call this living? Is this the best life has to offer? And to make our lives superficially better, to bring superficial thrills to our otherwise catatonic existence, we expand our circle of possessions rather than our consciousness. To us, expansion means growing through objects. And how much do these things really excite us? America is addicted to happiness through the impulse purchase.

But real excitement comes not from expanding our wallets but from expanding our minds and hearts. Expansion of consciousness happens when we reach a fever pitch of aliveness so potent that our brains blow a gasket. The limits of human understanding are pushed back.

In a truly erotic situation, one experiences sensory overload. The body's synapses are firing with such potency that the mind is totally overwhelmed by the depth and degree of sensual pleasure. The overload pushes the very limits of our humanity to breaking point, and it is that moment that we experience the malleability of being and the extension of human awareness. We are pushed into a higher sensory dimension. We never even knew that we could experience life at such high levels of intensity. The body, in its unaroused state, cannot contain such heightened stimulation. And it is at that moment, when completely aroused, that there comes to fruition a complete fusion between the detonator and the detonated—man and woman or woman and man—that the mind's boundaries are obliterated and one achieves limitless consciousness, seeing things that heretofore could not be seen, feeling things that previously could not be felt, understanding things that are normally outside the mind's grasp. This is

where the colors come in. One drinks in life in all its rich-
ness, experiencing the full spectrum of the soul's vibrancy.

The occurrence is rare, to be sure, but it is truly unforgettable, both for the man or woman who experiences it
and the spouse who brought it about and witnessed it. Such
heights of erotic consciousness cannot come about unless all
the ingredients enumerated above—innocence, novelty, the
chase, forbidden-ness, opposites attract, reckless abandon,
unquenchable yearning, and beyond the body—are present.
A mind-blowing experience like this could never happen
between two strangers simply because the emotional proximity needed to achieve this kind of liftoff would never be
present.

Expansion of consciousness means being completely present in the moment. Existence has sloughed away. There are
no distractions. You become completely aware of the energy
and the life-force that is your being and you experience unimaginable heights. Your body becomes a living Einsteinian
equation of $E=mc^2$, with matter being transformed into pure
energy. Few husbands believe that their wives are capable of
this level of arousal. They don't believe that the mother of
their children has that much energy tucked away. They look
at their wives as cooks and homemakers. But every husband
can serve as the detonator to bring out this erotic explosion
from his wife. And it's a good idea to do it before the pool
guy does it for you.

And when it's over, this expansion of consciousness becomes the gift that keeps on giving. You get to interrogate
your spouse about all the details of what they experienced at

that moment of supreme arousal. What did they see and hear when they went to the mountain's summit? What level of freedom and liberation did they find at the moment when the earth ceased revolving on its axis? What thoughts electrified their mind during this moment of expanded consciousness? This is a powerful erotic conversation. It mitigates a husband's need to ever find erotic thrills in some other woman. Compared with this kind of experience and the conversations it brings in its wake, porn is dead boring. Indeed, that kind of cheap eroticism becomes a turnoff to any husband when compared with witnessing his wife's erotic self explode. Pictures of naked women faking it become silly boys' stuff by comparison. The eroticism of men is the sexual fusion of a husband and wife, the erotic integration of masculine and feminine, generating such intense sparks, such massive friction, that a chain reaction is set in motion, with a volcanic, nuclear explosion leading to the melting away of all mental limitation.

This is no pipe dream. Every married couple can have it and couples that I have counseled have achieved it. You have to be careful to stick to a strict regimen. The previous seven ingredients must be present in your relationship. And there is one more ingredient that puts the icing on the cake: sex for a few nights in a row without climax. It's where you change sex from being a goal-oriented exercise into a means-oriented activity, allowing desire and erotic tension to build over a few nights until it finally detonates. We'll learn how to do this with a little help from our Eastern and Kabbalistic mystical friends.

Masculine and Feminine in Eastern and Kabbalistic Thought

*Let him kiss me with the kisses of his
mouth—for your love is more delightful
than wine.*
—SONG OF SONGS 1:2

*D*iscovering the mystical nature of sex provides great
assistance. I have criticized Western sexuality because of its
strong goal-orientation. In essence, we in America are taught
that great sex consists of great orgasms and, indeed, the whole
purpose of sex is to achieve climax. Sex is the means to the
higher end of sexual release, and a successful sexual encounter is one that always ends in orgasms.

Or is it?

Notice that in focusing on orgasms we attribute great value
to the powerful and pleasurable muscle contractions that are
the very essence of sexual climax. But note—the very word
contraction means to shrivel. Traditional orgasms are primarily about shriveling, squeezing the very desire for sex out of
our system. In such an experience, the pleasure of orgasm is
isolated in only one region of the body—usually the genitals.
True, a woman will sometimes experience pleasure in other
regions of her body, but frequently when the focus and goal of

orgasm is solely based on the presence of these contractions, then the pleasure is localized and the experience is halted once it has been achieved. Our desire for sex is almost literally squeezed out of our system. We satiate our erotic needs and then require them no more. Is this a good thing?

Contraction is perceived as pleasurable because it leads to an expulsion of tension, the purging of the body of built-up desire. But this is not the ultimate pleasure of which we are actually capable. All this pent-up sexual energy is then released suddenly, through the contraction of an orgasm. The result is a feeling that is pleasurable, as is all purging of tension. But the pleasure is fleeting. It is a pleasure that is localized, isolated, contained, and most of all, transient. Could it really be that this is as good as it gets? A ten-second orgasm? That's sex? That's the greatest pleasure known to us humans? Ten seconds! And of course, once the tensions go out of our system, we enter a calm state of mind and most often fall asleep. This is the whole problem with Western sexuality. It is focused on a ten-second prize that leads to sedation. No wonder men just run to the finish line. The reward being so infinitesimal, the effort is just not worth it.

Many have heard about Tantra and Tantric sex. Some know of it because the musician Sting is said to practice it. Others because they mistakenly hear that it can give you hour-long orgasms, as if anyone these days would even have the time (and your cell phone would ring in the middle, anyway). In reality, Tantra is an ancient Eastern thought system that seeks to explore spirituality through the physical. It is a holistic tradition based on the belief that the body contains divinity that can be accessed through sexuality. The main principle behind Tantric sex can be paraphrased in this way: people should live in a constant state of preorgasm. We are meant to harness sexual and erotic energy without allowing it to seep out, and utilize it in our waking, conscious life. In other words, unlike Western sexuality, Tantra is means-oriented. It is sex with the purpose of heightening arousal by delaying orgasm and not allowing your body to be purged of desire. You prolong sex for as long as possible in order to heighten the sensations that lead to the expansion of human consciousness. This sensation is then redirected, channeled into the mind, ultimately allowing us to live indefinitely in a heightened state of arousal. And that heightened state makes us live with unequaled vibrancy. When you live in a constant state of preorgasm, you don't get tired. You need very little sleep. Ordinary, everyday things become extraordinary. The natural begins to feel miraculous; the everyday, unique.

Mount Kilauea, a volcano in Hawaii, has been erupting since 1983 with no visible signs of cessation. My wife and I were awestruck to see the rivers of molten fire flowing from its summit. Yes, it is possible for a volcano to erupt for twenty-five years without a halt. Our bodies are like that volcano. Instead of feeling sexual only some of the time, we can, by not expunging our bodies of all our lava, feel volcanic all of the time.

The man or woman who practices a variation of Tantra, or what I call *Kosher Tantric Sex* can live in this heightened state. It involves utilizing Tantra without some of the more idolatrous connotations thereof, practicing it within the confines

of marriage, and adding an emotional and intimate compo-
nent. Doing so can have us live in a permanent state of erup-
tion, so to speak, building a fever pitch of erotic desire. We
can have marriages where we always feel deeply attracted to
each other and where we make love nearly every night.

By the time Meg and Danny came to see me, they had
not had sex in more than a year. Meg had put on weight, but
Danny denied that was the reason he did not feel like having
sex with his wife. He said he simply had not been in the
mood for many months. He complained that his wife bullied
him into it, made him feel guilty about not desiring her, and
that just diminished his interest in her even more. He said
he felt generally lethargic. It wasn't directed at his wife. He
just felt uninspired, like he had no energy. One comment he
made shocked me: "If my wife continues to badger me on
this sex thing, then I think I want a divorce." For her part,
Meg said that her husband not touching her at night was
torturing her. She felt ugly and unwanted. She wanted her
husband to be intimate with her. "We're not roommates, for
goodness' sake. We're married. This is unnatural." I told them
to start slow. "Meg, don't push your husband for sex. Rather,
when he comes home at night, massage his shoulders. Help
him relieve tension. Do that for a few days. Then Danny, like
any gentleman, you have to reciprocate. You should start by
massaging your wife's shoulders. From there the two of you
can progress to lying in bed and giving each other soft sensual
massages for a few minutes each night. If you feel like doing it
longer, do it longer. And if you then feel like you're desiring
each other more, slowly progress to more intense forms of

intimacy. But only if you feel like it. But here's the catch. Do not climax. Neither of you. As it is, Danny, your libido's running on fumes. So don't let any sexual steam leak out." They followed my advice. With a few hiccups, it began to work. After two weeks of touching each other, Danny wanted to have sex with his wife. They did so without climax, although both admitted it was challenging, and Danny had to leave the bed a few times to gain control. But he did it. They made it to a full week without either orgasming. Sex became long and involved, lasting more than an hour each time. Danny said that the hardest part of the exercise was that he could not sleep after sex. His body was still in a state of arousal. I said to him, "But isn't that good? Look how far you've come. A few weeks ago, you had no energy and no desire for your wife. Now, you have so much energy caused by desire for your wife that you can't even sleep!" The long sexual encounters were good for both of them. For Meg it was great exercise, a great calorie-burner, and most importantly, great for the ego and self-esteem. She felt like her husband loved her again. For Danny, it was an awakening from the dead. His shriveled self had begun to expand. And it wasn't only his sex life that was gradually restored, but his interest in the details of his life that had sucked his spirit out in the first place.

Sex is the ultimate expansion of one's life—of course, this occurs literally with physical arousal. Many things in the body expand (no, I won't elaborate), but it also happens figuratively, with the arousal and expansion of one's inner life. We expand like a sponge. It is at the moment of sexual peak that we are most able to take in all stimuli, and to take them in most fully.

Thus, the slightest word from a lover can either bring us to the highest ecstatic peak, or else to the depths of emotional pain—should the word be a careless or callous one. This is often named as the cause of female "anorgasm," a woman's inability to sexually climax. A man makes a snide remark about something strange that his lover says in the throes of passion, or the way that she looks in the throes of ecstasy, and the woman becomes completely cut off from that part of herself. She has absorbed fully and devastatingly the thoughtlessness of her lover. It can take years to recover, if ever.

But that is the negative side to our suddenly porous nature. The positive side is our ability to take in more than we are ever able to absorb, and thus, to fuse with our lover in ways that are not possible when the physical is not incorporated. In Tantra, there is an expression that captures the synthesis of male and female sexual secretions. It is called "astral fire." The bringing together of the masculine and feminine nectars creates earth-shattering sparks, qualities of which include the ability to house the creation of new life, as well as the creation of great passion.

That's the way it ought to be. We should all be reveling in amorous bliss. Sadly, however, for most husbands and wives it doesn't work that way. But why? Take the masculine, mix it with the feminine, and presto, you have a dish of great passion and intimacy. Who or what is throwing a spanner in the works?

Well, when G-d created men and women, he may very well have created them as equals in nearly all respects, but he did not create them *the same*. And where the differences are most pronounced is in the arena of sexuality.

Women are sensual. Men are sexual. Women are intimate. Men are detached. Women are fully experiential, employing every one of the five senses. Men are primarily visual, fixated on sight and appearance. Women are circular. Men are linear.

The differences are evident in every aspect of male and female sexuality. On the most basic level, when we look at the geography of the male body, we see that men are streamlined. They are angular and narrow, a straight line, curve-less until they hit middle age and nurture a belly, but they never develop hips. Their sexual organs are rigid, straight, simple, and narrow. Their pursuit is befitting their physical makeup—they size up their prey like an animal predator—and then "descend" on their "prey." In a dating situation, they advance and retreat like an army, their choices chartable along a straight line. Sometimes they pursue a woman with great vigor and gusto, advancing to make her their own. At other times, they feel trapped and claustrophobic, suddenly retreating from a relationship when they feel confined or are asked to make a commitment.

Sexually, anatomically, men behave true to their linear nature. The "curvy" nature of foreplay, for example, curvy because it means reaching coitus through a roundabout way rather than reducing sex to straightforward intercourse, comes only through instruction, and rarely instinctually. As men become more aroused, they actually become more linear. Even the orgasm is linear: semen shoots forward in a directed line.

Women's bodies, on the other hand, are built of curves and bends. They are designed to have hips and breasts. The female sexual organs are rounded, intricate, curvy, and complex. When a woman becomes aroused she becomes more circular. Her breasts and tissue swell. She becomes full. And of course, if she becomes pregnant, then she becomes even more curvaceous. For a woman an orgasmic experience is all about receiving, accepting, succumbing. Like a circle, it is about opening up and become more receptive. It is not about "seek and conquer." A woman operates in a fashion that is the extreme opposite of linear movement. She does not advance or retreat in a relationship, but rather slowly opens to a man who woos and closes to a man she doesn't trust. She is like the aperture on a camera, dilating or contracting, sometimes in an instant, other times so slowly that the movement is barely perceptible.

The female experience of sex cannot be an independent and detached one. Unlike a man, whose genitals are on the outside and can therefore treat sex as an out-of-body experience, a woman's sexual organs are on the inside, making it that much more difficult to compartmentalize the sexual act from the emotions. Studies have shown that in the act of intercourse, the female womb literally contracts to draw in the male sperm, increasing her chances for pregnancy. A woman's very body draws the male nectar in.

So how can such different creatures "make love'"? How can they enjoy sex together when their natures are so different? The answer is eroticism. Erotic fire melts and molds the two into one. When a man is electrified by a woman, he begins to ape her circular nature. Rather than being rigid and linear, the lines become a bit curved. He makes love in a more feminine manner. He does not rush into sex but savors his woman through the erotic pleasure of foreplay, which he prolongs as much as possible. He does not hold back his emotions but immerses himself into the act with body and heart. And he ensures that his wife enjoys the experience and climaxes first. He embraces her more curvaceous sexual nature, which might take a bit longer to reach a peak but once there remains there. Because unlike a straight line that can only go up or down, a woman's arc can remain at a sexual peak for much longer.

Conversely, as a woman becomes inflamed by the fire of erotic passion, she, too, melts into the experience and begins to assume some of the masculine traits. She is now not only open to sexual invasion by an occupying force, but welcomes it. She not only wants foreplay and a soft gentle touch. She welcomes intercourse because she desires her man to be a part of her.

I saw this most clearly with a couple I counseled while on a trip to Italy. Luigi had been with many women, but after meeting Stella he fell in love and wanted the relationship to work. Whereas before he had been inordinately masculine— pushing for sex on the first date, having sex be a pretty curtailed affair, and not being very emotionally responsive to the women he was dating—he was now a different man. A much more feminine man. Stella actually wanted to have sex fairly early in the relationship, and felt rejected when Luigi refused. He would kiss her passionately, they would engage in heavy petting. But he would always stop before sex. He didn't want this relationship to be like all the others. He wanted it to be special. He wanted it to work. It brought out all his nurturing qualities. He didn't want to use Stella, but take care of her. With Stella the exact opposite happened. She wanted to have intercourse because "I want him inside me. I want him to be as close as possible to me. I don't want kissing. That's not enough." Here I witnessed the reversal of sexual roles that erotic attraction can often bring out, which each, of course, misunderstood. Stella translated Luigi's reluctance to have intercourse as a lack of desire, when in reality it was precisely the opposite. And Luigi translated Stella's pressure for sex as a desire to keep the relationship physical rather than emotional, when in reality the opposite was the case. She wanted to be as close as possible precisely because the physical had become for her an expression of the emotional. My advice to them was to wait for sex until they were married. The delayed gratification would ensure that they didn't exhale the life out of their relationship before the consummation of real commitment.

But be that as it may, you now see why erotic passion is no luxury in sex. Without an erotic catalyst powerful enough to raise a man and woman above gender difference, what you get is two people who are sexually incongruous and who, as a result, have pretty bad sex.

This is where Eastern views of sexuality become so vital. Eastern sexuality is much more feminine than the Western variety. It is means- as opposed to goal-oriented, focused on connection as opposed to mastery, insistent on the harnessing of the emotions as opposed to the procurement of pleasure. What's even more amazing is that this means-oriented, energy-harnessing sexuality can have healing qualities as well.

Tantra believes that sexual energy heals and that this energy, called *Kundalini,* cures all the lesions of the body and the spirit through erotic envelopment. Eroticism is an electrical charge that makes men and women feel intensely alive. All disease is a product of a diminishment of life. Pain is caused by harm to the inner life-force. This isn't that difficult to understand. Just think of all the health issues caused by stress and anxiety.

It follows that healing comes from a restoration of the life-force, and eroticism is a charge that makes us feel intensely alive. Nothing makes us feel more vital, and nothing removes stress and anxiety more than love, eroticism, and romance. When we fall deeply in love we fall deeply into life. All the material concerns of the world peel away. To be in love is to have the colors of flowers magnified and the deep blue of the sky intensified. To feel deep erotic attraction is to have all the senses heightened. A man who is wounded by life, scarred and cynical by repeated setbacks, has his life restored to him through the power of attraction to a good woman and her reciprocity by loving him in return. The culmination of that erotic desire is causing sexual release in a woman through the power of intense arousal.

You see this happening in women who have affairs, like Elsa who came to see me about finding a way to end her affair with a colleague from work. It started because her husband was never home. Making money, rather than enjoying Elsa, was his real passion, and he was always on a business trip doing a deal. She taught second grade at school and started having lunch with a fellow teacher in the cafeteria. One thing led to another. It became a full-blown sexual affair. While we spoke, I got the feeling that she had come to me not get rid of her lover, but to alleviate her guilt. "To be honest, Elsa, it doesn't sound like you really want this to end." She thought for a moment. "Well, you're only partially right. I do want it to end. I know it's wrong. But I'm afraid of it ending. Before I met this guy, I was in pain. Every part of my body felt like it was sick. I used to get migraine headaches. My back hurt. My joints ached. I took so many pills. But now it's all gone away. Nothing hurts. Everything is exciting. I've discovered that rather than being an instrument of pain, my body can be an instrument of pleasure."

Because of this feeling of euphoria and seemingly healing powers of an affair, an increasing number of authors are suggesting that adultery can be good for you. Balderdash. You don't solve the complications in your life by adding the biggest complication of all. And you don't overcome depression by immersing yourself in the kind of sin that is only going to lead to more guilt and more depression. It's not the affair that is bringing the euphoria, but the healing power of romantic love and sex. And you could have had it with your husband. You could have, in the words of the subtitle of my *Kosher Adultery* book, "turned your marriage into an affair." And if your husband refuses to ever get it, if he refuses to change, then worse comes to worst, get a divorce. But you don't become healed from the scars of life by inflicting the scars of deception and fraud on your own soul.

The release of highly potent sexual energy is enormously therapeutic. This is true on an emotional and spiritual level and in the physical sense as well. We are very tense before sex and we are very relaxed afterward. Sex has phenomenal physiological, psychological, and emotional benefits. But it also has spiritual benefits, because it leads to a feeling of transcendence. A husband and wife who really connect in a moment of sexual passion are transported to a higher place, away from the cares of the world. They no longer feel like they are in two distinct bodies but have become one. To be spiritual is to transcend the confines of space-time reality, and for many of us the most potent manifestation of this phenomenon is the unity we attain during lovemaking.

People are in pain when they are alone. But an intense erotic connection ensures that they are forever connected. A deep erotic connection between husband and wife makes them feel like they are together even when they are geographically separated because they are always on each others' minds.

I have employed the biblical terms to describe husband and wife as "bone of one bone," and "flesh of one flesh," all of which is true in a metaphorical sense. But in reality, they are two, distinct people. Amazingly, however, the power of sexual release is a feeling of being melded and merged into one. Distinctiveness disappears as they become entangled into one heaving mass, the product of intense love and desire. Well after sex is over, they still cleave to each other and fall asleep in each other's arms.

Men need women in order to heal physically, mentally, and sexually. A woman is the healing energy that is absolutely essential to a man. She is his comforter, who takes away his pain. The Bible put it best, "A man who has found a woman has found goodness." She is a warm bath that soothes every ache and soreness. The pleasure that a woman gives a man is unlike anything else he will ever know. That's why a woman is so sensually beautiful to a man, and making love to a woman is the most glorious experience for a man. But it can only be done with real commitment and love. This healing can never come from an abusive relationship where a man simply uses a woman to satisfy an urge.

Men today are not finding the healing they once got from women because they have dehumanized them and reduced them to a collection of body parts. In bed they do not receive that healing because, rather than letting go of themselves in sex, they become a Supreme Court justice in bed. They are detached and condescending. The mind never shuts off. He evaluates her rather than falls for her. She takes off her clothes and he becomes a plastic surgeon, suggesting she could do better up here and lose a bit down there. "Compared to other women I've been with, her breasts seem pear-shaped rather than round. Her legs are kind of short. And what is all that cellulite?" Cheap premarital sex has eroded the male ability to be healed by a woman because men have unfortunately become, through overexposure, experts in a woman's body, an area where expertise actually undermines desire.

Erotic attraction is where the calculating mind is shut off and the visceral self takes over. Because men don't let go completely, because they don't allow a woman to have their heart, they can enjoy none of the real benefits of genuine emotional closeness and intense erotic desire. There simply isn't enough openness. It is usually a man trying to make an impression on a woman, trying to seduce a woman, overpower a woman, instead of letting go and with an open heart worshipping the feminine.

This is what happened to Matt who, after being single until age forty-one, finally married Claire. Strangely, however, he did not find himself strongly attracted to his wife. No matter, he told me, they could be best friends. He married Claire for her mind and because she was so easy to get along with. Oh, and he also by now wanted to have children. I told him, "Don't blame Claire for what is essentially a deficiency in you. You're the one who had tens of girlfriends before you married. You're the one whose mind has amalgamated them all into one perfect package. And you're the one who cannot help but compare your wife to that false image of perfection. When you and your wife get into bed, your mind is supposed to turn off and your heart is supposed to turn on. But you get in with all these mental images of women who have preceded Claire. And as the Talmud says regarding people who remarry but cannot forgo the mental image of the previous spouse, that's a pretty crowded bed."

Sex, in Tantra and Kabbalah, is a tool for expansion. Consciousness expands as the heart and body swells. But for Matt, his heart condensed and his horizons became restricted. He felt less love for his wife after they married.

We know that things like barbiturates, marijuana, and alcohol can lead to mind expansion. But they come about artificially, through ingestion of a foreign substance. The expansion also doesn't last. Indeed, when the artificial high wears off, they actually lead to a contraction of mind and heart. That's why drugs and an overindulgence of alcohol, aside from being destructive and toxic, are a bad idea. The mind expansion that comes with sexual ecstasy is much more powerful, and natural, not artificial. It is not contrived, but organic and intuitive. And most importantly, it is not ephemeral; it is continually working.

This idea of the feminine healing the masculine is taken to an extreme in Tantra, so much so that the exchange of bodily fluids is seen as an essential part of that healing. Indeed, there are Eastern sects that treat a woman's sexual zone as the paradise of Eden and her sexual secretions as the fountain of youth. To be sure, even if we don't subscribe to such flowery language about the female body, this is the way a husband should feel when he is with his wife, that gaining pleasure from her body helps him to enter Eden, and that his wife, and his wife alone, holds in her body the keys to his personal paradise.

Imagine the kind of marriages we would have if husbands worshipped their wives to this extent, if they focused every ounce of their erotic attention on their wives. We would do away with adultery and divorce because a man would feel utterly bereft without his wife.

Now, in my book *Kosher Sex*, I dealt with the permissibility, from a biblical and Jewish-values perspective, of oral sex. I deduced that so long as a man does not intentionally destroy seed, there was nothing wrong with a husband and wife trying a new sexual repertoire, including oral sex, that would bring them greater passion and intimacy. This does not mean that a man must embrace the Tantric practice of directly using feminine secretions as a form of healing. But what is clear is that if a married couple does choose to make oral stimulation a part of their sex life, if a husband shows a disgust for that part of his wife's anatomy, it is better not to engage in it in the first place. To be sure, Judaism does not ascribe any healing powers to a woman's sexual secretions. But it does advocate sex as the ultimate form of knowledge and intimacy. So, what is certain is that a man should never treat his wife's body as something distasteful. Indeed, sex has an incredibly transformative power, whereby things that might, outside a sexual context, appear bizarre or even painful, become a source of joy and pleasure in the sexual congress between husband and wife. If that transformation has not taken place, and couples still feel, during sex, that they are doing things that are repulsive, you can usually bet that this is due to a lack of passion and a failure of the erotic to take hold of the participants.

It is also important to note that amid the similarities between Kabbalah and Tantra, there are undeniable and weighty differences, the most significant of which is that Tantra can be construed as involving direct idol worship and is associated with representations and manifestation of pagan gods. Since Judaism is passionately monotheistic and wages an intense war against any and all forms of idolatry, this aspect of Tantra becomes highly unkosher. In culling insights from Tantra into intimacy between husbands and wives, there is a need to strip away all of the pagan overtones. Tantra does often rest on a fundamental pagan premise of many gods. But the similarities I point out are unconnected with these pagan principles that are anathema to all who believe in the one, indivisible G-d. It is therefore the secrets of eroticism, rather than the implementation of Tantra, from which we can learn.

Kabbalah, like Tantra, rejects the idea that sex is a purely physical act. Rather, sex uses the physical to arouse the spiritual and mystical. The moment of sexual climax that follows extreme arousal leads to an opening of the mind and heart, which allows another person to enter, resulting in unimaginable degrees of closeness and intimacy.

But in order for these intimate qualities to be realized, great time and energy must be committed to the sexual experience. Since couples rarely allow for much foreplay, and most have a minimal understanding of the human body, and of human sexuality—especially female sexuality—they rarely achieve this physical ecstasy. For most couples, sex is about two bodies that produce friction rather than one body produced by an intimate act. The one-soul, one-body objective of sex can only be achieved by first fanning and fueling the erotic mind. The real purpose of foreplay is to stoke the fires of desire and lust. Only when a man yearns for his wife with all his might can he become one with her. He cannot have any other outlet. The sexual consciousness of husband and wife is aroused by having foreplay without sex, and sexual intercourse without orgasm so that lust and desire are fostered. The Talmud goes to great lengths in emphasizing the need for a husband to "celebrate" with his wife prior to sexual penetration. Sexual congress should not be had without first stoking the fire of desire. Indeed, Judaism makes it a grave sin to use one's wife's body for pleasure without her enjoying the experience as well. Her pleasure is paramount.

Kabbalah seeks to uplift the physical by infusing it with transcendent holiness. This is especially true of the sexual connection between husband and wife. This will become more apparent in the next chapter which delves into what I call *Kosher Tantric Sex*.

KOSHER
TANTRIC SEX

Love is the answer; but while you are
waiting for the answer, sex raises some pretty
good questions.
—WOODY ALLEN

*K*abbalah is the esoteric tradition and the mystical
soul of Judaism. Its principal work is called *The Zohar, The
Book of Radiance.* The written works of Kabbalah seek to explore the essence of existence and divinity. Kabbalah posits
that there are hidden divine sparks latent throughout creation. Thus, all creation is holy. Sex is holy. The heat created
between husband and wife is holy. Kabbalah seeks to uncover
the hidden unity that underlies all creation. Things appear
to be different, but they have a foundational godly nature
all the same. Hence, Kabbalah utilizes a great deal of sexual
imagery. In showing the mystical connection between G-d
and his world, the Creator and his creation, Kabbalah makes
use of extensive sexual metaphors. These metaphors are very
detailed, with even human anatomy being used to describe
the interaction between the lofty *heichalot,* spiritual universes,
and divine emanations. There are mystical energies that give,
and there are mystical energies that receive.

The union of the opposites of husband and wife becomes the prime arena for demonstrating the ultimate unity of G-d and his creation.

The literal meaning of the word *Kabbalah* is "to receive," and indeed the Kabbalistic tradition and its practitioners seek to transform all aspects of the physical world into receptacles for holiness. Kabbalah believes that the greatest light can be brought to the darkest of places and that human beings should seek to illuminate the very places where godliness seems to be nonexistent.

Tantra is an ancient Eastern thought system that some believe is derived from the Vedic tradition. The literal translation of *Tantra* is "weaving" or "web," as the Tantric tradition recognizes a spiritual continuum, where the lines between physicality and spirituality are nonexistent, and where the world can be seen operating as an indivisible matrix of energy.

Although both Kabbalah and Tantra derive from different mystical traditions, they share some striking similarities.

The essence of Kabbalah is a belief that hidden sparks of spirituality reside within every fiber of material existence. A spiritual undercurrent underlies the husk of physical reality. It is the objective of Kabbalah to reveal it. G-d can be found everywhere. Kabbalah therefore dismisses utterly earth-heaven/mind-matter/body-soul dualism that is so prevalent in world religion. Kabbalah, true to the Jewish tradition of which it is a part, is passionately monist as opposed to dualistic. The body is no less holy than the soul. The earth is not subordinate to the heavens. G-d can be found in the coarsest physicality just as he can be found in the most ethereal spirituality. Hence,

sexual imagery is not frowned upon in the Kabbalistic understanding of the nature of G-d, which posits that G-d has
both a feminine and masculine energy. The feminine aspect
of G-d is the Creator, giving rise to the universe from the
cosmic womb. The masculine aspect to divinity is the more
rigid G-d of history, who rewards the righteous and punishes
the wicked. Sex, the ultimate unification of man and woman,
is used as a metaphor for the absolute connection between
these two divine energies, as well as G-d and the creation.
Since sex is about the joining together of opposites, as it per-
fectly connects masculine and feminine, it thereby captures
the nature of G-d, which blends together all existence, even
those which appear to be polar opposites.

Tantra believes the same. Whereas many have understood
Hinduism, Buddhism, and other Eastern disciplines as call-
ing for the denial of the pleasures of the flesh and the abro-
gation of attachment to the senses, the Tantrics emphasize
desire, passion, and ecstasy as central to spiritual enlightenment. Tantra agrees that humans should never be ruled by
desire; to do so would be to live imprisoned by the flesh. But
Tantra advocates that desire could be mastered by immersion
rather than escape. Desire could be channeled into a passionate appreciation for life. Tantra encourages us to dive deeply
into the ocean of passion and promises that by doing so we
gain pearls of enlightenment. Just as Kabbalah believes that
spirituality can be unearthed from all places and enlightenment can be culled from all experiences, Tantra is especially
insistent that sexual intimacy has the power to expand the
mind and grant unique insight. Sexual immersion became

a major paradigm of Tantric ritual and meditation. In short, sex can be used not just for procreation and pleasure, but for personal insight and the expansion of consciousness. Sex does not consist merely of the act of penetration, but the act of two energy bodies rubbing against one another and generating first heat and then enlightenment. Tantra allows for the maximization of sexual pleasure because, by doing away with guilt and fear, it breaks down the self-imposed walls that serve to separate male and female even in the sexual act.

Karen and Bob were married for four years. Their sex life was a nightmare. Bob suffered from erectile dysfunction brought about by performance anxiety. Karen could never enjoy the experience because it barely lasted, while for Bob it was even worse. He felt like a failure and was sure his wife looked down at him. I told Bob that he should, of course, seek medical remedies. But aside from treatment, he had to do away once and for all with his sense of inadequacy and guilt. Sex had become for him something akin to the Olympics. He was sure that his wife sat there with a scorecard, giving him ones and zeroes. If he let go and stopped trying to *do*, in bed, and instead just tried to *be*, things would go much better. "Stop being a stud. Just be a husband. You don't even need to have regular penetration. Expand what you understand sex to be. Make it more encompassing, more holistic. It's kissing, hugging, breathing, touching, kneading, petting."

Both Kabbalah and Tantra teach the importance of familiarity with our mystical nature. The deeper we delve into our truest spiritual selves, the more our limitations and boundaries dissolve, letting us enter into new realms of awareness.

It follows that the more our limitations disappear, the more capable we are of true sexual ecstasy and togetherness. We become empowered and more fulfilled. Tantra teaches that the orgasms we experience in this state of expanded consciousness are exponentially more explosive and potentially unending than in a lesser, more limited state.

It's a simple equation. When are you more apt to have better orgasms? When you're at home and thinking about all the bills you have to pay, or when you're on vacation and haven't a care in the world? Orgasms are dependent on an elasticity of mind. Pressure kills them completely.

Jimmy and Alyson came to see me, both looking worn and depressed. It turned out that, try as they might, Alyson could never have an orgasm from her husband. He tried everything, but it didn't work. "What's on your mind, Alyson?" I asked her. "Nothing much. Just the usual. We have three kids. They are a lot of work. So much work. I never knew it could be that much work." I told them, "Okay, this is what you're going to do. I know you don't have a lot of money. But whatever money you were going to spend on a family vacation, you're going to instead spend on getting Alyson three hours of daily household help. Better to have a nightly vacation and find pleasure in each other's arms than have a harassed wife who gets to be off for two weeks out of the year. Second, put the kids to bed by nine thirty at the latest. After that, your marriage is a function-free zone. There is no discussing anything functional. Not the kids' schools, not the laundry, not things that have to be fixed around the house. Clear your minds of all those pesky subjects so you can just be a man and a woman again, the way you were when you were dating, and the erotic sparks will start coming back. And so will your ability to climax."

Both Kabbalah and Tantra maintain that there is a life-energy that courses through the universe and pulses through each individual man and woman. Great sex is reflected in the ability to tap into that life-energy and submit to it freely. Sex not only expands consciousness, but it can also liberate it so that it colors our everyday experiences.

In Tantra, sexual energy is something to be harnessed rather than suppressed. Kabbalah does not deny sex; just the opposite, it embraces it. Both Kabbalah and Tantra maintain sex is sacred and not a sin.

Human beings must seek to merge with, rather than withdraw from, sexual energy. By merging with our sexual energy, we in turn become one with the universal energy. Tapping into deep erotic yearning is the means by which we tap into the life-force of the world as it courses through the universe.

Kabbalah explains that sex is sacred because it involves the union of opposites, a quality that mimics the duality of G-d. The antipodes of male and female come together as one, thereby demonstrating the inherent unity of creation. The ancient Greeks and Romans may have believed in male and female pagan gods. Their mythology is laced with stories of Zeus and Jupiter, Hera and Aphrodite. Indeed, even Eros features as the Greek god of love with his Roman counterpart being the even more famous Cupid. But while the Kabbalah acknowledges a masculine and feminine dimension in the Godhead—the G-d of history versus G-d-the-Creator; the

G-d of justice and discipline versus the G-d of love and beneficence—it strongly emphasizes that these are dual dimensions of the same, indivisible, one G-d. Hence, the union of masculine and feminine, of man and woman, of husband and wife, is the ultimate manifestation of the oneness and unity of the Creator. It is in this light that the sublime and holy nature of matrimony is to be considered. When man and woman marry, they create the transcendent mathematical equation of one plus one equaling one. They join together becoming bone of one bone, and flesh of one flesh.

In Tantra, too, sex is used as the cosmic union of opposites. There is a primordial energy in the universe. Sex, with its polarity charge of masculine and feminine, taps into this universal polarity and connects with the primordial energy from which everything arises in the universe.

There is enlightened and unenlightened sexuality, the basic difference being that unenlightened sexuality is merely physical and is divorced from the soul and the mind. It leads to no expansion of consciousness. Indeed, it leads to human devolution as men and women succumb entirely to instinct and make sex into an animal exercise. This unenlightened sex is incarcerating and leads to all the unhealthy addictions that we see in the sexual realm, from porn addiction to womanizing.

Both Kabbalah and Tantra speak of sex as a prolonged engagement involving deep and penetrating intimacy. In Tantra, sex is prolonged through the delayed gratification of deferred orgasm. You learn to prolong the act of making love and to focus on, rather than dispel, potent orgasmic energies moving through you, thereby raising the level of consciousness.

Brian and Jennifer told me during counseling that the most erotic experience they ever had together was when Brian once stimulated his wife manually with the great in-and-out pressure that left her gasping for air. She began screaming, although she was not even aware of it. Brian was convinced that the force of his action and shoving his fingers into her private regions with such force was causing her pain and he stopped. She took his hand and ordered him to continue. He had never seen his wife in such ecstasy. When it was over he asked her to describe what was happening. She said, "Normally, you stimulate me with your hands until I orgasm and it feels great. But then it's over and I feel exhausted from the intensity of the orgasm. But what you were doing now was the strongest combination of pleasure and pain. I felt sensations going through my whole body all the way up to my brain. It was so much more powerful than usual. It was like tiny little orgasms that came every second. They wouldn't stop. I felt like you were taking over my whole body, like I had no choice but to submit, both to what you were doing to me and also to the mini-orgasms that were taking over my body. These orgasms had nowhere to go, so they just stayed inside me and gave me even greater pleasure. It was the most pleasurable thing that ever happened to me."

Tantra transports sexuality from simply doing to actually *being*. There is no end goal in Tantric sex, only the present moment of an ideal, erotic union. In this respect, it is extremely different from Western sexuality with its emphasis on valleys and peaks. Tantra says you can remain at a peak level for days or even weeks. There is no need to come down from the mountain.

Both Kabbalah and Tantra are feminine disciplines, emphasizing the superiority of the feminine to the masculine. As I said earlier, in the act of sex, the masculine is enveloped by the feminine; the line is encompassed by the circle. It is the feminine that has the upper hand. Yes, men are goal-oriented and women are means-oriented. In bed, men are focused on climax and orgasmic pleasure and women are more focused on the intimacy and closeness engendered. Great sex is where both passion and intimacy come hand in hand.

Bobby and Susie were in counseling with me about what they described to me as the worst crisis in their seven-year marriage. The core problem was that Bobby no longer desired sex with his wife. He said he was depressed about business and it had shot his libido. His wife pressured him repeatedly for sex. He said that it led to cataclysmic arguments, with him accusing her of not being sensitive, not being understanding of his feelings. "She's become a sexual bully. All she wants is sex. She is manic. And I just don't feel like it. She should leave me alone. Her desire for sex is all about her. It's selfish." Obviously, those of you reading this are probably surprised at this turn of events. It's normally the husband who wants it more than the wife. But I had seen this scenario a thousand times, especially in our day, the era of *The Broken American Male,* a phenomenon to which I devoted my last book. In our day, certainly, women are much more sexual than men. Men often feel like failures and are uninterested in sex, preferring instead to watch TV and follow sports. I told Bobby, "You're missing the point. You think your wife wants sex for selfish pleasure, and you accuse her of not being understanding. In truth, she wants sex to feel closer to you. She feels you pulling away and she translates it as a rejection of her. From your perspective you don't want sex because you're depressed. But from her perspective, you don't want sex because you don't want her. You don't feel attracted to her. And this isn't like not wanting to eat her cooking, where you reject the caterer in your wife. Or not wanting her advice about business, where you reject the businessperson in her. No, when you don't want to make love to your wife, you're rejecting the *woman* in her, her deepest essence. And that's why she's badgering you. She's a desperate woman. You have made her feel utterly unwanted. Because, whereas for you sex is about passion, and right now you just don't feel it, for a wife, sex is about intimacy. And sex in marriage is supposed to provide for both."

Both Tantra and Kabbalah view humanity as being created in the godly image. Sex therefore becomes an act of worship of the divine spark in the other. The body assumes a mystical and holy dimension. Tantra teaches you to worship your sexual partner and to transform the act of sex into a sacrament of love. Lovemaking is a spiritual endeavor and mystical journey. If sex is accompanied by a deep and soulful awareness, it becomes a gateway to spiritual ecstasy and heavenly consciousness.

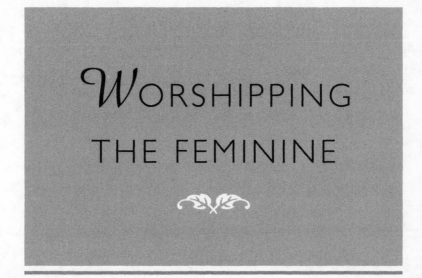

WORSHIPPING
THE FEMININE

I never realized until lately that women were
supposed to be the inferior sex.
—KATHARINE HEPBURN

Of all earthly endeavors, only sex grants the possibility of man and woman merging the dual nature of their respective beings into one indivisible sexually ecstatic experience. This is the goal of Tantra and a primary teaching of the Kabbalah.

As sexual beings, we have the ability to raise the spiritual energy within ourselves and use it to experience mystical states of consciousness. In effect, we become "gods" of our own bodies. Hence, so much about Tantra is about the worship of the feminine as a god. It is about the masculine worshipping the feminine. In practical terms, this means a husband coming to worship his wife's body and focusing intently on her response to all the sexual activities he initiates.

With rare exceptions history has unfortunately produced the opposite: the feminine worshipping the masculine. Throughout the ages, it is women who were taught to look up to, and be dependent on, men. Masculinity was held up as the model of greatness to which all should aspire. It remains so today. We live in a male world where conquest, acquisition, career, and other male specialties remain the gold standard to which both men and women aspire. But in the hustle to get ahead, the truly fundamental feminine qualities that serve to balance the masculine have been relegated to second-class status.

This was not so in times of yore, specifically the court of Eleanor of Aquitaine, mother of Richard the Lionhearted, in Provence, where courtly love began. According to the ideals of courtly love, a woman was seen as an unattainable prize, an exquisite treasure high above man's reach. The effect of women being placed on a pedestal was that men had to work hard to be thought worthy of a woman. Winning a damsel was a lifelong pursuit, and a man would spend his days refining his character in order to win the fair lady. Knights would produce feats of great daring, all designed to impress and capture the hearts of the women they loved. Even after marriage, a wife maintained her status as a lofty creature to whom the husband devoted himself to please.

The ancient rabbis declared in the Talmud that the worth of a man is determined by how he treats his wife. An honorable man, they said, was a man who dressed his wife in far better clothing than he himself wore. Having his initials on his collar meant nothing compared to the wedding ring that told the world that so glorious a creature as a woman was prepared to accept him as a husband. Marriage, therefore, was the ultimate sign of status because every time a man married, it was like marrying into the nobility. Wearing $5,000 hand-tailored suits was immaterial but decking his wife in noble attire was a marker of his own achievements. The ancient rabbis also said that greeting a woman was like greeting the divine presence. When Moses first encountered G-d in the desert, he was commanded to take off his shoes lest he trample on holy ground. Chivalry, too, was once predicated on the idea that men had to mind their manners in the presence of creatures who reflected the divine spirit. The firm belief in times of old was that it took feminine sanctity to create masculine dignity.

This ideal carried on so that as late as 1936 the world applauded King Edward VIII for forfeiting a kingdom of 600 million subjects, and a quarter of the world's surface, for the love of a single woman. Today, of course, wealthy businessmen routinely dump the devoted wife for the young, loose social climber with a boob job. Unfortunately, Western women are letting all of this happen, closing their eyes to the dangerous trend before them, all in the name of not wanting to be patronized as being superior.

But long ago, both Tantra and Kabbalah established, without wanting to patronize, that the masculine should be worshipping the feminine. Men needed to become gentler, more companion-like and less competitive. They needed to truly adore their wives and get along with their peers. They had to learn from female sacrifice. Taking on a nurturing role and allowing others to shine was not unmanly but heroic. Likewise, in sex, men had to become more feminine and learn that real sex is a sharing of the self with a soul mate. The masculine had to soften and pay homage to something more feminine.

Hence, the worship of the feminine is central to both Kabbalah and Tantra. In Tantra, *Shiva*, the masculine, worships *Shakti*, the feminine, which, although in Sanskrit, bears a striking resemblance to the Hebrew word for the feminine divine presence, *Shekhinah*. Yab worships Yum and Yang is superseded by Yin. Likewise, in Kabbalah *za*, the masculine, celestial spheres, reaches its apogee by joining with *malchus*, the feminine, creative spheres.

Tantric sex is a deeply feminine form of sex, focused not on the friction of body parts, but on the union of souls. Tantra often demands sex without climax, sex bereft of the masculine insistence on immediate gratification in favor of prolonging the journey of closeness and togetherness.

There is so much that can be gleaned from Kabbalah and Tantra in fostering eroticism. Unfortunately, both are viewed as mystical disciplines that remain largely inaccessible to average people. Each is shrouded in mystery. And yet, each has enjoyed a resurgence in popularity in the past several decades. What is it about Kabbalah and Tantra, amid their obtuse mystical nature, that appeals to our twenty-first-century sensibilities?

What is central both to Tantra and Kabbalah is a belief that a man and a woman are each, individually, the embodiment of a divine energy. A man is the embodiment of masculine divine energy and the woman is the embodiment of the feminine divine energy. Both also maintain that the feminine energy is superior because she represents life and the power of creation. Thus sex becomes, first and foremost, the process of worshipping this feminine life-force. That's why, almost naturally, the man takes the lead in sex in trying to stimulate the woman. The masculine arouses the feminine. Ergo, when a man makes love to a woman, both Tantric and Kabbalistic guides structure sex as a physical enactment of this intense worship and complete veneration. And when a man brings a woman to climax, he is releasing the explosive divine energy that resides within. The same is true in the mystical realm, where the Kabbalah explains the masculine spheres "build up" the feminine sphere of *malchus*, until, reaching a critical mass, it detonates and, analogous to the big bang, the universe is born.

A man's objective during sex is to instigate the vibration in what is the natural stillness and passivity of the female. His goal should be to get *her* to vibrate. Hence, the arousal of the feminine is paramount. In Kabbalah, the feminine is called *malchus*, and *malchus* gives birth to the universe. But to do so it first has to be built up, it has to be aroused. The celestial spheres above *malchus* all contribute to that building until the feminine explodes with a universal life-force that is creation. Likewise, here in our terrestrial world, the "building up" of the feminine is paramount. And in the marriage between a man and a woman, the husband "building up" his wife, first through ongoing romantic gestures and compliments and later through intense sexual arousal, is what allows the two of them to reach intense sexual heights. This is true in the most straightforward sense. Sex in which a man focuses only on his own pleasure is boring beyond belief, for the woman, of course, but for the man as well. But it's the kind of sex that is most commonly practiced in the American bedroom and accounts for why sex, on average, lasts about five minutes. Slam, bam, is that all there is, man?

When this point of vibration is achieved, both Kabbalah and Tantra maintain, the feminine creative energy is released. It is akin to an explosion, and when this energy is finally liberated, it not only vastly excites, but brings redemption and vast healing to the masculine. A man is redeemed through the intense love and caressing given him by his wife, especially when he pleasures her sexually. The release of the feminine nectar brings healing to a man.

Once a woman orgasms she releases her feminine nectar, her feminine essence. And when a man orgasms he releases his masculinity, and they blend together—that is what we mean by the "astral fire," the synthesis of masculine and feminine elixirs.

In other words, during orgasm we both become a sponge; that is why we cling on to each other so tightly during orgasm—we are absorbing the other person's essence. We are drinking in their most vital selves. It is our most vulnerable moment, and that is why the sense of touch is so explosive.

He brings out a quality in her that is previously dormant. He is granted the great privilege of sharing his life with a woman of incredible vibrancy and erotic attractiveness. He is also rendered immune to the charms of other women, since no other can compare. Which really begs the question, why do husbands not make the effort to bring this quality out of their wives? Why do they diffuse their sexual focus by succumbing to their need for variety when, if they focused intensely on their wives, they would be blown sky-high with delight? There is no good answer except to invest your energies in that vertical, rather than a horizontal direction. Overcome your inclination to take the easy, lazy way out that has so little reward.

SEX WITHOUT CLIMAX: AN EXERCISE

Having established that both Tantra and Kabbalah believe that the way to enlightenment is through the body, then the next point of interest is how we set out to bring out the full potential of ecstasy of which the body is capable. Both Tantra and Kabbalah provide tangible exercises that aim to release these energies.

According to Kabbalah, man is the sun and the woman the moon, so she reflects his light. He lusts after her, making her into an object of intense desire and focus. He shines, in effect, all his light on her. She, in turn, reflects that light back. She gets "turned on" by his attention, becoming radiant as he stimulates her and helps to release her nascent erotic energy. It is the light that shines on her during sex that is reflected back.

If foreplay is extended long enough, if the breathing and intense staring is prolonged, then a husband and wife can achieve a very heightened state of erotic arousal. In this orgiastic state of inner and outer expansion, a couple achieves a heightened state of extrasensory perception, allowing the man and the woman to have true, nonverbal communication. They begin to intuit each other and understand each other on the deepest possible plane. This is what the Bible means when it refers to sex as knowledge. Some ideas are so deep that they cannot be expressed in words. This is certainly true of the spirit, which is too lofty to be contained by vowels and consonants. The real language of the soul is love, and the true melding of the male and female spirit is attained through the nonverbal communication of sexual congress.

In everyday life, only the externalities of the human personality are revealed. The outer husk of ourselves is what we share with the world. But in sex our deepest essence is revealed. Outer and inner clothing, husk and inhibition, is discarded and our quintessence is uncovered.

So orgasm should ideally involve a timelessness and a total dissolution of the ego, where you dissolve into each other. It is where your subjective sensations of being are absorbed by your spouse.

Orgasm should also involve an opening of the eyes, peering deeply into the soul of your spouse as you climax and enter the realm of higher consciousness. Studies show that most men and women closer their eyes during sex and especially during orgasm. This is a lost opportunity for fusion and intimacy. In essence, your desire should be to bring your spouse along with you. Or better, into you. And how can you do that if you close your eyes?

These exercises revolve around worshipping the feminine. A husband should be totally focused on his wife's body and bring her to an elevated state of arousal. He should focus on cycles of seven in creating the proper erotic environment. The most mystical of all numbers is seven. There are seven days of the week, connoting the natural order and the divinity contained within. According to the Talmud there are seven heavens. And according to the Kabbalah, there are seven emotions of the heart: 1) benevolence/love; 2) might/discipline; 3) harmony/beauty; 4) victory; 5) splendor; 6) foundation; and 7) majesty. There are also seven primary *chakra*s, or spiritual centers, which, in Eastern thought, are said to be conduits for life-energy. These are root, sacral, solar plexus, heart, throat, third eye, and crown.

As we practice the following ancient Tantric exercise, which is based on the number seven, we connect ourselves to the wider creation, the heavenly host, and the intimate emotions of our spouse.

That includes waiting seven days before full sexual penetration takes place.

As I delineate the following exercise, which is extremely rewarding, although not all that easy to accomplish, let's lay out three user levels. We'll begin with expert, which in this case denotes a husband and wife who are having sex on a regular basis, say, about five times a week, but who find it a bit predictable and uninspiring. Second, we'll tailor the exercise for the intermediate, which connotes husband and wife who are at the national average, say, having sex about once a week. Finally, we'll amend the exercise for the beginners, that is, those married couples who have not had sex in three months or more and who really need to start all over.

The "expert" husband should begin the process on the first night, Saturday night, the beginning of the biblical week, by giving his wife a long erotic massage. The proper way to proceed is to see the body as being comprised of a series of seven concentric circles. First, there is the outer circle. For the first night, for two hours, he lightly touches her hair, eyelids, eyebrows, ear lobes, toes, hands, feet, and nose. He can also use his breath to lightly blow on her, especially her ears. Effort must be exerted to resist the temptation to go further. Let desire build.

On the second night he focuses on the second, more inner circle. He should touch her legs below the knee. On her hands he focuses on her fingertips all the way to her elbow. He should turn his wife on her side, the side of the body serving as a body-length highway that he should stroke with his fingers. He should also stroke her neck.

On the third night he penetrates more deeply, focusing on the third circle, which consists of her inner thighs, her knees, and the area under her knee. He should stroke and caress her elbow, on both sides and touch her arm from the elbow to the shoulder.

On the fourth night he goes for the fourth circle, consisting of her armpits, breasts, stomach, back, and buttocks.

On the fifth night, the fifth circle: her genital area.

On the sixth night, her clitoris and G-spot, simultaneously, as well as massaging her nipples.

Looking at this mystically, the human body is said to have two poles: there is a masculine and feminine within a woman and a masculine and feminine within a man. In a woman, the external clitoris is said to be the masculine pole and the internal G-spot is named as the feminine pole. To successfully pursue the stimulation process for a woman it is necessary for the man to stimulate both these regions simultaneously. Simultaneous stimulation of both the positive and the negative poles within the woman is a practice that is frequently neglected, but, according to Tantra, is essential to arouse a woman fully. Simultaneous stimulation of both poles together creates unbelievable sparks of intensity.

On the seventh night, Friday night, the sacred Sabbath, when an extra measure of holiness is present and there is time for lovemaking since there are no physical distractions—no work to be done, no worries about finance—it is time for spiritual and sexual intimacy. After the buildup of the entire week, after all the arousal that comes from six consecutive nights of increasing intimacy as more and more of the circles are penetrated, it is time for ecstasy. The seventh night is the time for the seventh and innermost circle, the circle of complete physical unity that comes about through intercourse and penetration where couples become bone of one bone and flesh of one flesh.

And then the cycle begins again, on Saturday night, and slowly builds up to its culmination on the next Friday night.

For the intermediate couples, the routine should be as follows. Make it three nights instead of seven. On the first night, focus on the two outer circles of your wife's body. On the second night, focus on the two circles that are inward from there. And finally, on the third night, preferably Friday night, focus on the remaining three. Begin with a long sensual massage of your wife's sexual zones, continue to manual stimulation of her genitals, and climax with sexual penetration and oneness.

And for you beginners out there, husbands and wives who have not had sex in many months, focus on just two nights. On the first night massage her erogenous zones: back of her neck, inner thighs, earlobes, buttocks, elbows, and knees. But no sex. Arouse her, and arouse yourself by watching her. And on the second night, move from her erogenous zones to her sexual zones: breasts, genitals, culminating in sex. In all three cases, if you can have sex without climax, prolonging penetration for an hour or more, so much the better. If it means stopping when you feel yourself about to climax and withdrawing, then by all means do that. When you've lost the desire to climax, start again. And if you can stop completely after an hour without either of you climaxing and shifting all that erotic energy to your waking state the following morning until you can resume again at night, so much the better. You will be living in an ecstatic preorgasmic state. Your energy levels will be higher, and nervous tension will propel you through your day. And, best of all, you won't be able to wait to see your spouse at night. They will feel intensely desirable.

For wives the same three user levels apply. After your husband has spent a week, or three days, or just two, giving you these ecstasy exercises, practice the same thing on him. Use the same description of the seven circles as it applies to his body. Oh, and use your imagination, women being so much more sexually imaginative than men.

Many husbands will complain that this cycle is unworkable, even impossible. Are they really supposed to touch their wives for a whole week without sex? Are they really supposed to control their own urges as they build up the sexual desire in their wives?

To be sure, this takes serious discipline, and you must develop a sexual rhythm, which works so as not to achieve orgasm. But it is doable and when you try it, you'll immediately feel the rewards.

And why do all this? Because if you go through this process for an entire month, you can jump-start any relationship. Even the most moribund marriage will be resurrected by stoking the flames of desire into a towering inferno. For all those husbands who feel like they're not attracted to their wives, or who feel distracted by other women, when you practice this kind of desire building, their lust for their wives will build to a crescendo. There will be a resurrection of dead desire. Likewise, their wives' desire will reach such a peak that they will yearn for their husbands every moment of the day. Most importantly, the couple will begin to live erotically. Eroticism will influence and inform every one of their actions. Even as they go to work and do household chores, they will have added energy as their craving and lust for each other informs and inspires their day. They will not need as much sleep, will not get as tired, and will feel filled with energy.

While the idea that the husband and wife should have sex without climax (and we know how goal-oriented men are) may sound pretty crazy, there are plenty of other ways to experience sexual pleasure and closeness without climax. Indeed, very often the opposite is true. As soon as sexual gratification is had, the sexual urge is lost. Hence, creating a period of weeks where the lust builds up without release is essential to creating an erotic paradise of desire that is filled with an unquenchable, raging fire-lust for one's spouse.

Rather than focusing on sexual gratification and climax, husband and wife should substitute intimacy. Work on drawing closer. They should keep their eyes open and kiss each other, creating the three-pronged unity of one life-force (breath of life exchanged through kissing), one spirit (eyes-open sex, the eyes being the window to the soul), and one flesh (entanglement of limbs in sexual togetherness). Kabbalah is adamant that sex has as its principal feature this overall goal of total fusion and harmony.

Couples should go through this cycle for four weeks. Only on the fourth week should they actually have sexual release and orgasm. By this time, they are living with a truly expanded consciousness. They are living in permanent lust for each other. There is no possibility that a husband will have to think about another woman in order to stimulate himself while having sex with his wife. Rather than the three erogenous zones (two breasts and genitals) that are the tiny domain of the American male's view of a woman, a direct consequence of the de-eroticization of the female body through overexposure, every part of her body will become erotic to him. They will hunger for each other as a man hungers for water in a parched desert.

This is the kind of love glorified so beautifully in Song of Solomon: "Sustain me with raisin cakes, refresh me with apples, because I am lovesick" (2:25). Again, in chapter eight, Solomon says, "Many waters cannot quench love, nor will rivers overflow it; if a man were to give all the riches of his house for love, it would be utterly despised." Here he is talking about this highest level of erotic desire, where a husband and wife want each other so profoundly that there is nothing else in life that could possibly satiate them. Here is a level of desire that a husband develops for his wife for which no pay raise could compensate and for which no Ferrari could substitute. He desires her more than money and fame. He lusts for her more than a yacht or the presidency of the United States. This is true love—what the Kabbalists call the fire-lust—and so few ever attain it.

Expanded consciousness also derives from the heights of erotic desire that is thereby attained. The little things that we lust for in life, objects rather than people, TV rather than our spouse, disappear into ignominy as one's spouse becomes the all-encompassing object of desire.

And at this level of lust, you no longer see yourself as an entity distinct from your spouse. You become one and the same with them. The distance between the two of you disappears. So, too, all of life is seen through a prism of enhanced awareness and consciousness. Colors become more vibrant, emotions stronger and more pronounced.

Many make the mistake of believing that love rather than lust is important in a marriage. In truth, both are absolutely essential. The husband who does not lust after his wife insults his wife. In effect, he is saying to her, "I love you, but I don't want you. I cherish you, but I don't *need* you."

A few years ago there was a story about an evangelical Christian woman from Texas who was organizing Tupperware-style parties to sell marital aids to enhance passion between married couples. She was arrested on indecency laws in Texas and was also expelled, along with her family, from her church. I debated the Reverend Flip Benham of Operation Rescue in North Carolina about her case on the radio. Flip, who is a friend, was adamant that what she did was immoral. He condemned her actions. "But, Flip," I asked him, "what's wrong with bringing lust into marriage? Marriages die without lust." Flip responded with a critique. "I feel sorry for your wife Shmuley, if you have to turn her into some object that you lust after. You're supposed to love your wife, not lust after your wife."

"If that's correct," I responded, "then why does the Tenth Commandment say, 'You shall not covet your *neighbor's* wife'? It should have said, 'You shall not covet *any* woman.'" Clearly, the implication is that while you should not be lusting after your neighbor's wife, you should definitely be lusting after your own." Lust is holy in marriage. G-d wants us to lust after our spouse, and marriage without lust is a lifeless corpse.

ADDITIONAL EXERCISES

Here are other exercises that can be used by husbands and wives to enhance lust and magnify eroticism.

1. Mutual breathing in a position whereby the wife sits astride her husband, but without penetration. Husband and wife can even be wearing clothing during this exercise, and sometimes it's advisable to do so in order that the

exercise not become sexual. One breathes in, the other breathes out, creating a circle of life. You have to be very disciplined. You cannot let yourself go further. Breathing should go on for at least a half hour. You must peer deeply into each other's eyes while doing this. No speaking, just breathing—but eyes must remain open.

After you've done this for a few nights in a row with clothing, you can then graduate to doing it naked. Whatever happens after that is your business, but don't rush it. Let desire build through breathing.

2. Men need novelty in order to stimulate eroticism. Many husbands pursue the need for eroticism in a sinful fashion by thinking about other women while making love to their wives. Just think about how bizarre this is. Here he is, in the closest physical proximity to his wife, and in his mind he is doing a guest appearance on "America's Next Top Model." It is an utter abuse of the relationship. This is utterly unacceptable and is a sin against the intimacy of marriage. Rather, when he feels he is not sufficiently attracted to his wife, a husband should imagine his wife with other men in order to spark his erotic desire. This is especially true of men whom he already suspects she is attracted to. When he perceives her as she really is, as every woman is, a man's dream, when she becomes the locus of male desire in the general sense, his own desire is rekindled. He should also ask his wife, in order to spark erotic interest, about the men to whom she feels attracted. This must, of course, be

done with patience and gentleness in order for his wife to open up. In all these exercises, the purpose is for his wife to come alive to him as Eve incarnate, the primordial woman, the universal embodiment of male desire.

3. A husband should spend a good half hour kissing his wife's breast, and while doing so, treating it as the fountain of life, as the spring from which flows all sustenance. And this should not be limited to the breast, of course. Kissing her mouth is the exchange of life-breaths and the ultimate intimate act. By drinking in her life-breath, she becomes the spiritual source of his sustenance. But while kissing her breast, he should think to himself that his wife's body is the source of his healing. She alone, among all nurturers of the world, possesses the power to make his aches go away.

4. A husband should find out how his wife wants to be touched. He should go over her whole body, repeatedly asking her what brings her the most pleasure. He should know every contour of his wife's body deeply and intimately. Make sure you get her to respond: "good," "great," and "incredible" are good descriptions to encourage her to use, commensurate with the level of her enjoyment.

5. To expand on a very intimate exercise mentioned above, couples should spend an hour staring into each other's eyes, and using their eyes as a form of nonverbal communication. They should say things to each other through the eyes alone. Then, they should play a guessing game of what

the other is saying with these intimate gestures. Nonverbal communication with the eyes works because the eyes are the window to the soul. With practice, they come to know each other's deepest thoughts through the pupil of the eye alone.

6. A man should tell his wife, detail by detail, what he wants to do to her, how he wishes to touch her. He should whisper it in her ear or talk softly to her while looking directly in her eyes. This also works well when they are geographically apart. It becomes a very erotic phone conversation that heightens desire until they reunite. Tell her what you plan to do to her when you arrive home. Then it's the wife's turn to say what surprises she has planned.

7. A husband should give his wife long foot massages, paying special attention to each individual toe. In Kabbalah, the feet are part of the divine sphere of *yesod*, foundation, which is related to both the sexual organs and the feet, *siyuma degufa*, the extremities of the body. Massaging the feet provides direct stimulation to the genital region and is a most effective way of arousing libido without being directly sexual. The results are explosive. And your wife will love you for the effort. So will your husband if you lovingly reciprocate.

Bringing it all together, an ideal sexual encounter would begin something like this: the couple would first get into the lotus position and would just stare deeply into each other's eyes for half an hour. Ideally, they would still be clothed during the breathing exercise. Next, they would begin breathing in unison, practicing alternate breathing as discussed above. He would take in a breath and she would exhale a breath, until they developed a continual circuit of life-breaths. As they do this, they would envision the exchange of breath going in a never-ending circle of unity that brings them together. Breath is, after all, the very basis of life. Soon, they are encompassed by a circular energy that joins them together.

They would then get into what is known in Tantra as the Yab-Yum position. The man sits in the lotus position with his legs crossed and the woman sits on top of him. They begin without sexual penetration, and both are still wearing clothing. This would be done on three consecutive nights to heighten desire and create a circle of intimacy based on breathing and staring deeply into each other's eyes. The man and woman hold each other, and they continue the breathing exercises. The idea here is that they are slowly expanding sensual bandwidth. Prior to the protracted exercise, they might have thought they were only capable of a limited spectrum of feeling. Now they begin to experience heightened sensations that take them to another level. Slowly, their minds expand as well. They feel more alert, more aware, and more connected. They become "conscious soul mates," feeling joined at the hip even when separated. Their bodies feel like one amid any distance. They are two wings of a single bird, incapable of elevation without the antithetical propulsion provided by the other.

On the next night, the clothing comes off and they give each other long sensual massages, bringing desire to its apogee. And finally, they make love, beginning one flesh and one spirit. But they delay climax for a few nights in order to remain in that heightened state of arousal. Far from this program being merely about sex, they begin to be of one rhythm, internalizing each other's inner vibrations. What one feels, the other feels. What one experiences, the other experiences. They feel and are inseparable.

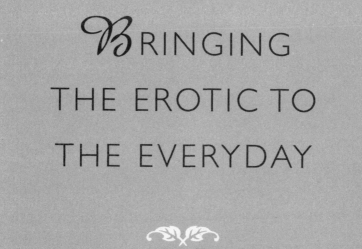

BRINGING THE EROTIC TO THE EVERYDAY

For one human being to love another; that is
perhaps the most difficult of all our tasks, the
ultimate, the last test and proof, the work for
which all other work is but preparation.
—RAINER MARIA RILKE

$\mathcal{T}$he erotic need not be localized to the bedroom. It need not be confined to the carnal. We can live our lives with the same erotic pulse that is the hallmark of physical love. We can overcome the boredom of the everyday and the monotony of routine by imbuing life with a healthy erotic pulse. We can extrapolate from the sexual to the nonsexual areas of life, imbibing them all with an erotic current. A reimagining of the sexual experience can bring eroticism into our everyday existence. The intense curiosity of the erotic can impregnate even the minutiae of daily life with passion.

So many things that we take for granted, like the falling rain and howling wind, should evoke within us a spirit of majesty, awe, and wonder. Nature has limitless depth. When we remove its external veneer we become aware of its erotic delights. It draws us in and we are mesmerized. Prayer is a focused meditation on the sanctity in all that surrounds us. Awaken yourself to its power. Look for and find the divine sparks that animate earth. Drink it in; delve into its mystery.

Every day, I try to take a walk into nature, be it summer or winter. There is a wood near our home and I walk among its trees and creek. It connects me with innocence, opens my eyes to transcendence, and allows me to be immersed in something divine. Being in nature opens my eyes to the limitlessness of existence. When I am in nature its erotic essence opens up to me and all boredom goes away.

I hate exercising. Hate it. I know I have to do it. But the idea of walking to nowhere for an hour on a treadmill is excruciatingly dull. But I can walk ten miles in nature and, thank G-d, rarely get tired. I am awed by what I see.

But exercise is not the only thing that gets to me. I also dislike mornings. I am a night person, staying up late, talking to my wife, composing essays, reading magazines and books, writing e-mails, and writing books. I dread the mornings. The first thing I think of in the mornings is not the glory of being but the innumerable tasks the day brings. I think of the millions of things I have to do, the endless responsibilities of life, and I don't even want to get out of bed. But that's why morning prayer becomes so meaningful. It steers my mind back to the wonder rather than the obligations of my life. It offers life an erotic charge. Prayer awakens me to life's blessings rather than its burdens. And walking in nature does the same. I can't stand being cooped up in concrete. It crushes my spirit. Nature is where I come alive. I return phone calls while I walk in the woods. Doing so while being incarcerated at a desk is purgatory. In summer, I sit with my laptop out on the porch. We ought to get rid of offices. Human beings should be productive. But they are not designed to spend their lives chained to a desk. Modern technology is gradually making that possible.

Read the newspaper every morning, but read it differently from the way you are accustomed. Don't read to find out what's going on in the world. That's betrays an addiction to horizontal renewal. You're bored with your life, so you read the news. What terrible thing happened last night that can provide some entertaining news today? Rather, read it with a view toward fathoming human nature. What makes people tick? What makes them do the things they do? Focus on questions rather than answers. Go deeper. Use changing events to spark your erotic curiosity. For example, you open the paper and you see that the Democrats and the Republicans have been fighting again over some issue: a Wall Street bailout, immigration, taxes. But this isn't only about Mexicans crossing the border or a portion of your earnings going to the government. It's about power and a game of one-upmanship. Human beings are stirred by the desire to feel significant. It's about wanting to be right and feeling vindicated by the other party being wrong. Politicians in both parties desire recognition, and they seem to achieve it by gaining power at the expense of the other. Which does not mean that one party isn't, indeed, right and the other, indeed, wrong. It just means that there are forces at work here beneath the surface that you are should strive to understand. Read the news with a view toward understanding how human nature propels people toward wanting to distinguish themselves. People spend their whole lives pursuing recognition. Might this account for why educated, professional people would bicker in such a way that it is often unbecoming and at times downright degrading? You read about how a celebrity went off the deep end by getting drunk and driving their car into a tree. They're arrested and they're going to jail for a month. Normally, this would be great watercooler talk. A bunch of envious, "ordinary" people taking pleasure in discussing the downfall of a star. But look at it very differently. Everyone wants to be famous. So why are those who've achieved their dreams so darn miserable? They should be happy instead of depressed. So why do they drink themselves into oblivion? And don't give clichéd answers: "because money doesn't make you happy." We know that already. Could it be because the greatest necessity of being human is having dignity, and somewhere along the line, in order to become famous, they might have compromised that dignity? Could it be that what we all seek in life is the validation that comes from being loved, but these people have substituted love for attention? We all wish to have our humanity distinguished; we all wish to be special. But attention is not the same as love. Can it be that dignity consists of something other than being recognized on the street? It doesn't even matter whether your insight into human nature is the correct one or not. What does matter is that you are beginning to peer beneath the veil, looking under the hood of life. Ordinary stories become extraordinary as the mystery of life slowly reveals itself. Far from being routine, life is unpredictable, forbidden, and full of surprises. You are now peering into someone else's soul. And it's deeply erotic.

I have a lot going on every day. But after morning prayers I start the day by dipping into the *New York Times,* the *Washington Post,* and the *Wall Street Journal.* I don't read just to cull information. If I wanted simply to know what's going on, I would watch the evening news. No, I read to understand life. To obtain a snapshot of the world's soul. I read to understand human nature. And I walk away enriched and excited by the experience. The earth and its inhabitants are fascinating.

This is especially true of texts that are much deeper and erotic than the newspaper, especially the greatest of all works, the Bible. There is no book on earth where God is more sparkling, where great personalities come to life, where sex is more erotic, or that provides deeper insight into the magic of creation and the workings of human nature. The Bible tells the story of men and women who, in their effort to meet their creator and achieve transcendence, became archetypes and whose actions invite endless probing and investigation. No book makes one more curious. No book fires the human imagination like the Bible. That's why I study a portion of the Bible every day.

As I go through my day, I try to bring the very same introspection that I bring to the world on to myself. If I start the day lethargic, I don't just accept it. I try to understand it. *Why do I feel uninspired today? What's eating away at me? Why am I getting frustrated so quickly?* Truth be told, I sometimes start the day feeling fearful. *What's bothering me; what am I afraid of?* I ask myself. What I don't do is simply brush the emotions aside. Every feeling I have provides an opportunity for self-discovery. If I'm agitated and easily provoked, I put aside pat reasons, like the fact that I'm tired and therefore irritable. I do things for a reason, and I want to understand why. *What is the source of my insecurity? What makes me feel inadequate?* Can I strip back the layers of my soul in order to fathom my own essence? I don't want to be boring even to myself. And then, if I discover something insightful about human nature, I try to share those insights with the people around me, creating a deeper and more personal working environment. If I understand why I do the things I do and I share it with others, it calls forth from them a deeper attachment as well.

Take, for example, my propensity to get easily frustrated. Frustration comes very quickly to me, and I have never completely cured myself of it. It would be easy to simply say that I am impatient. But that would be shallow, clichéd, and would lend me little in the field of self-understanding. So I dig deeper.

I am awash in insecurities, many of which go back to my childhood. I was raised in a home with little stability and I absorbed much of the chaos that surrounded me. So I try to prove myself. I get frustrated because, lacking a secure foundation at the core of my personality, I feel like I'm sinking if I fail. Every professional endeavor is an opportunity to prove that I have value. And if the endeavor fails, then the possibility lurks that I am a failure. So I sweat the small stuff. When you are fighting for your survival, there is no small stuff. It's all big stuff. And if life doesn't go according to plan, it tugs at the heart of your existence. The point behind all of this is simple. I refuse to let life bore me. I try to understand myself and thereby heal myself. Life has an erotic, curious quality that I try to grab by the horns.

This is especially true when I come home at night. After the kids are in bed, I usually share with my wife not only what happened to me that day but how I felt about what happened. I find myself baring my soul. The insights I garner about my nature I try to share with her to garner her feedback. It's a safe zone to discuss my inner demons. This is, after all, my wife and soul mate. Shouldn't you do the same with your spouse rather than just watch some dumb sitcom together?

Be sinful. As you bring depth and insight into life, you are addressing one of the key ingredients of eroticism: curiosity and knowledge. But in order to be erotic, it has to be sinful. You dare not allow your life to descend into monotonous predictability. But less so can you become someone who breaks the law and, say, takes drugs in order to be destructively sinful. You also can't cheat on your spouse because you have failed at bringing passion into your marriage. That's not the kind of sinfulness that will enrich your life. Rather, erotic sinfulness is based on something completely different. It's what I call "radical individuality." Everything around you tells you to conform to a social norm. Being part of society means learning to fit in. You are supposed to look like everyone else, think like everyone else, and be like everyone else. But then there are those rare individuals who buck the trend and refuse to conform. They don't look to be different. They simply look to be themselves. Not because they want to make a point or be a rebel without a cause, but rather because they refuse to erase their individuality. G-d did not make them better than anyone else. But he did make them different. And different they shall remain.

The ability to safeguard, promote, and protect their uniqueness amid being immersed in a society that is about conformity is that which makes them sinful. They say what they feel, even if people find it unacceptable. They follow their inner convictions, however unpopular. They do as they please in accordance with their deeply held value system, rather than merely succumbing to some animal impulse. To do so would not be sinful. It would be natural. No, they say what they mean and mean what they say, with little social filter. And they couldn't care less who raises their eyebrows. Nonconformists are sinful because they buck what others deem acceptable. They are erotically charged and they have magnetic personalities not because they are blessed necessarily with charisma but because they are radical individualists. He or she is almost always the most interesting person in the room.

I'm, of course, not advocating that you be a nonconformist simply to stand out. We're not looking for a rebel without a cause. Rather, I'm advocating that you be yourself and break away from the pack because you are intrinsically different. Find your uniqueness. Identify your gift. Never allow your individuality to be erased. To paraphrase Abraham Lincoln, the tragedy of being human is that all of us are born G-d's original, but most of us die man's copy.

This is the reason why women love bad boys. They are the ones who are usually the most authentic. They are individuals and exhibit a "devil may care" individuality. That kind of rugged individualism is super-attractive to women. Now, sadly, often they're also not the best people and their nonconformity often exhibits itself in the form of a flouting of basic rules. There is certainly a need to conform to basic standards of goodness, decency, and civility. But after ensuring you're a good person (because that also accords with your deepest nature), your sense of humor, sense of purpose, and sense of self should all be your own. Go ahead. Be different. Be sinful.

Find novelty in all things by going deeper. Finding something new does not mean that you have to always *do* something new. Earlier I dwelled on the difference between horizontal and vertical renewal. Vertical renewal is the ability to find something new in everything you experience because you peel away the layers, uncover the depth, and discover something novel. So dig deeper. Into yourself. Into the world around you. Read books that make you think more deeply. I love authors like Erich Fromm, Victor Frankl, Joseph Soloveitchik, and my Rebbe and mentor, Rabbi Menachem Schneerson, all of whose works penetrate the outer layers of life. When you finish reading their books, you look at life differently. It's richer, deeper, more profound. Things you thought you knew are now seen in a new light. Religion also provides that deeper insight into life by demanding that we strip away existence's outer veneer. Religious Jews, for instance, read the Bible in a cycle every year. The same stories are taken to a new level each and every cycle. We delve deeper into the character of Abraham, the leadership of Moses, the songs of David, the courage of Esther, until these personalities come alive with incredible originality and vibrancy. Then, we are able to bring those insights into our own lives, allowing us to reinvent ourselves with greater texture, foresight, and of course, erotic interest.

Conclusion

The tragedy of sexual intercourse is the
perpetual virginity of the soul.
—WILLIAM B. YEATS

When I was in my teen years studying to become a rabbi, I came across the verse of the Bible where G-d says to the Israelites, "For my law is not something empty from you." Commenting on the tortured syntax, the Talmud suggests, "If G-d's law feels like it's something empty and boring, then know that the emptiness comes *from you.*" I think of that verse often. I think of it when at times I find my life boring, my job boring, my marriage boring, or being a parent boring. All those things are in reality fascinating. Endlessly fascinating. The emptiness comes *from* me. I am the boring one.

That has been the essential message of this book. Everything around you is electrifying. If it feels stultifying, then the emptiness comes from you. The solution is rediscovering your inner erotic charge. Eros is the human ability to rediscover infinite curiosity in every thing under the sun.

The history of humanity is a history of insatiability and discontent. For us humans, the grass is always greener on the other side. We rarely appreciate what we have and focus instead on what we lack. We seem not even half full. We run on empty. Our lives are dull, and we employ an endless variety of meaningless escapes to fill in the blank spaces. There is a belief that adventure somehow lies just outside of us. If only we could retire in our thirties and permanently travel. If only we could be rich or famous. If only we could look like a model. If only, if only . . . and in the process of this endless wishing, we fail to appreciate what we have, squander our potential, and never end up becoming what we might otherwise be.

There is a better way. We humans are capable of taking that which seems to be ordinary and making it extraordinary. We are capable of taking the everyday and making it unique. We can take the natural and make it miraculous.

The secret lies in living the erotic life. We can impart erotic curiosity to the most seemingly mundane moments and give our lives a pulse. Like a magician who can take an ordinary hat and bring forth from it wonders, we can take the ordinary cloth of our lives and infuse it with splendor.

I have counseled many married couples where the chief complaint was boredom and a stultifying routine. In many of these cases, it was the husband complaining that he no longer found his wife sexually exciting and aesthetically attractive. What he was really saying was that he no longer found his wife erotic. Eros had been lost, not from her but *from his perception* of her. Restoring his erotic view of her was often as simple as having him witness the attraction that other men had for her, or having her reveal her fantasies about other men to him. Through these experiences, while his wife remained the same, he came to see her in a totally new and erotic light. And what before had bored him now excited him. What was really necessary was for the husband to recognize that the emptiness he felt in his marriage actually came from within. It was he who was the culprit, rather than his wife. The same is, of course, true with a wife who finds her marriage uninspiring. Yes, there may have to be serious changes in order to reinvigorate the relationship. But one of those changes is going to have to come from within.

The same is true with virtually every other area of life. I know many people who find nature utterly unappetizing. They prefer the acquisition that can be had in a shopping mall to the wonder that can be found in a mountain range. When they look at a leaf they see the boring color of green. It cannot provide something that can fill them up the way that a new dress or a new cell phone can. But in the lost ability to experience natural wonder, their humanity, their connection with the universal life-force, has been compromised. What is needed is a return to the erotic. As a man longs and lusts for a woman, so, too, we can have experiences in nature that awaken our desire to shed the artificial layers created by civilization and return to an invigorating, natural state. Whether it is the awe-inspiring event of witnessing a moose with her cub walking in the woods, as I have seen with my children, or an endless number of turquoise-blue glaciers snaking down the slopes of Mount Rainier in Washington State, nature has the ability to awaken the erotic. Once we have had this experience, a shopping mall can never compare.

The same is true especially of knowledge. There is an erotic quality to knowledge that makes us want to know. I remember a friend who was hopelessly addicted to movies tell me that when she saw *Titanic* she suddenly wanted to know everything about the ship's disaster and spent many nights reading books and articles on the Internet about those who were lost and those who survived. Within her there had been a transformation. Whereas before she was satisfied with any shallow story that provided a mindless escape from what she perceived to the be the drudgery of her ordinary life, once she found a story that truly engaged her, she had an unquenchable thirst to know not fantasy, but the real human story. And what was it about that particular movie that so sparked her interest? It was its mystery. The combination of the silent sea, the silent dead, and the conundrum of how an unsinkable vessel could be lost on its maiden voyage, all came together to create a powerful erotic spark. Where there is mystery, the erotic thrives. Where there is something hidden, the erotic can paradoxically be revealed. And where there is depth, the erotic can be manifest.

This book is a first step. You must continue from here. There are no excuses to lead a life devoid of inspiration. It is time for us to recapture our erotic fascination with other people, our marriage, our spouse, our children, and the rest of our existence. It is time once again to live a magical life.

Acknowledgments

Gideon Weil of Harper One flattered me with his kind comments about my previous books and my TV and radio show from our first conversation. It's both a pleasure and an honor to have an editor who believes deeply that I have something important to contribute. G-d bless you, Gideon. I hope this book lives up to your high standards.

Oprah Winfrey gave me one of the great honors of my life by inviting me to join her distinguished group of broadcasters on *Oprah and Friends*. There are few human beings alive who have more influence than Oprah, and there are few who deserve it as much as her. From being arguably the most philanthropic of all celebrities, to encouraging her vast following to live for others, to her celebration of the American family, to finding spiritual purpose, read books, and perform acts of kindness, Oprah's life is a sanctification of all that is blessed.

Ahuva Rogers, my family's dear friend from Detroit, edited this manuscript and gave me lots of great ideas. Ahuva is a naturally deep spiritual and insightful woman and was instrumental in giving the book a strong, sequential order and a more holistic exploration of eros. Before Ahuva began, I was under the impression that one could not improve on perfection. But lo and behold, she has! Thank you Ahuva and G-d bless you.

John Gehron, Laurie Cantillo, Charles the lawyer, Megan Robertson, Geneen Harstok, and all my colleagues at Harpo radio are dear friends and great sources of inspiration. I love working with you guys. It's an honor. You teach me, inspire me, and make my daily broadcasts a joy and delight.

Chris Martin and his wife Jenna actually came up with the title for this book. If it succeeds wildly, it is because of the content. If it fails miserably, the title is definitely to blame. I love you both and thank you for being such good friends. Chris's colleague at Harpo, Candi Carter, is also a wonderful friend whose constant encouragement always inspires. Candi is the greatest wife and mother to her beautiful son, Emerson.

Jason Kitchen, my friend, colleague, and assistant of more than two years, ran my office and looked after many joint enterprises so that I could do things like write books on eroticism. Jason, you have indirectly brought passion to millions of moribund marriages across the United States. Babies will be named after you.

Kennia Ramirez, my trusted assistant, spares no effort to gain control of my professional life and make it orderly and smooth. Given that I'm usually firing on many fronts, it's a herculean challenge that could test the patience of a saint.

Luckily, Kennia is a saint, a nice Catholic girl who oversees the professional life of a rabbi. Who knew? Dean Bigbee runs my online presence so that billions of people the world over can buy a Shmuley bobblehead.

My parents, Yoav Boteach and Eleanor Paul, are my heroes and have always inspired me. I am forty-two as of this writing, but I still always seek and receive their approval, wisdom, and encouragement.

My brothers and sisters, as I say in all my books, are my best friends. Sarala, Bar Kochva, Iris, Chaim Moishe, and Ateret, thank you for always being there. And thanks for all the wedgies you gave me when I was younger, which have kept me humble, meek, and unable to sit properly.

My children are my light and joy. Mushki, Chana, Shterny, Mendy, Shaina, Baba, Yosef, Dovid Chaim, and Cheftziba, where would I be without you? Probably with a lot more money, traveling the world, and downing fine single-malt whisky. But it just wouldn't be as much fun waking up in the middle of the night to change a diaper with a present inside. You illuminate my life. You uplift me, inspire me, and keep me young.

My wife, Debbie, is my soulmate in all things. We have just celebrated our twentieth wedding anniversary, thank G-d. Okay, so I celebrated it and my wife endured it. But you get the point. How this woman has put up with me is one of the great stories of courage in the annals of human suffering. But she clearly welcomes living martyrdom. This is as much her book as it is mine, and if it fails miserably, then it is much more hers than mine.

Finally, G-d Almighty has always loved me, blessed me, enlightened me, and restored me to a righteous path. Thank you, Lord. I am not worthy, as we both know. But I'd be grateful if you continued to overlook that and light my path and be at my side. It's an honor to try to live a life that is in accordance with your will. And I'll try to show my deepest appreciation by devoting my life to your work. There is no more noble pursuit.

Rabbi Shmuley Boteach,

New Jersey, November 2008